THE FRENCH COOKIE BAKEBOOK

François Franke

And

Blanche Thomas

In collaboration with Mindful Publishing

D1319417

Mandinettes (small almond cookies)
Serves 4

Preparation time: 10 min

Ingredients

200g almond powder
200g brown or wholemeal sugar
4 egg whites
2 teaspoons of almond flavouring

Preparation

Preheat the oven to 180°.
Mix the almond powder and the sugar to obtain a homogeneous mixture.
Beat the egg whites until stiff and fold them gently into the mixture, taking care
not to break them (they will give the cookies their lightness and softness).
Add the almond flavouring and pour into small individual moulds.
Place in the oven immediately and let cool for a few minutes before serving
with a custard or panacotta.

Praline Muffins
Muffins: 12

Preparation time: 20 min

Ingredients

200g of pralinoise
2 eggs
220g of flour
100g of sugar
1 packet of baking powder
10cl sunflower oil
15cl semi-skimmed milk
1 teaspoon of vanilla extract

Preparation

Preheat the oven to 200°C (thermostat 6-7).
Mix the flour, yeast and sugar in a bowl. Mix the milk, eggs, oil and vanilla in another bowl.
Then mix the two preparations together to obtain a homogeneous mixture.
Melt the praline in the microwave and add to the mixture.
Fill the muffin tins 2/3 full.
Place in the oven for 8-10 minutes (to melt) or 12-15 minutes (for softness).

Muffins, praline and nuts
muffins: 12

Preparation time: 15 min

Ingredients

200g dessert praline (one bar)
220g flour
100g of powdered sugar
1 packet of baking powder
2 pinches of salt
2 eggs
60g of walnut kernel
15cl of milk
10cl of oil
1 teaspoon vanilla extract

Preparation

Preheat your oven to 200°. Mix the flour, yeast, salt and sugar.
In another bowl, mix the milk, eggs, oil and vanilla. Make a well in the floured preparation, add
the 2nd preparation and mix it all together to obtain a homogeneous but a bit grainy dough.
Add the chopped walnuts. Melt the praline with a little water and add to the batter.
Fill your muffin tins or ramekins 3/4 full with butter and flour and bake for about
15 minutes at 200°. Your muffins should still be soft in the middle.
Let them rest for 5min, and unmould them. Bon appétit!

Philadelphia and Speculoos Dessert
Serves about 5

Preparation time: 10 min

Ingredients

200g of speculoos
75g butter
150g of Philadelphia
10 spoons of water
1 lemon juice
2 packets of vanilla sugar
8 tablespoons of fine sugar
20cl of fresh cream
3 sheets of gelatin

Preparation

Grind the speculoos into fine crumbs and mix this powder with the melted butter.
Spread this mixture in a muffin tin (preferably silicone) for individual portions
or in a cake tin for a cake. In fact, any pan will do.
Soak the gelatin leaves in water, add the sugar and let melt over low heat.
Mix the cheese with the lemon juice and vanilla sugar and add the cooled gelatin-sugar mixture.

Beat the cream and add it to the mixture.
Let stand for at least 6 hours in the fridge.
Turn out and serve as is or with a raspberry coulis.
Bon appétit!

Chocolate bavarois on a speculoos crisp
Serves 6

Preparation time: 30 min

Ingredients

200g of speculoos
80g of butter
200ml of milk
3 egg yolks
45g of sugar
200g of caramel chocolate (Nestlé dessert type, you can mix several kinds)
200ml of sour cream
3 sheets of gelatin
20g of powdered sugar

Preparation

Soak 3 sheets of gelatin in cold water.
Melt the butter, crush the speculoos, mix and put in the bottom of the mould and put in the fridge.
Heat 200 ml of milk.
Mix the egg yolks and sugar until the mixture turns white.
When the milk is hot, add the egg yolk and sugar mixture and heat again (do not boil) until the mixture coats the spoon and thickens a little.
Remove from heat and stir in chocolate pieces.
Add the drained gelatin and mix well until it disappears.
Whip the whole cream with a little powdered sugar.
Add the whipped cream to the chocolate mixture.
Place in a springform pan or pastry circle.
Set in the refrigerator for at least 2 hours.

Peach and vanilla speculoos verrines
Serves 6

Preparation time: 3 hours

Ingredients

200g of speculoos
90g of butter
3 peaches
10g of sugar

Preparation

Mousse to be made at least two hours before.
For the base :
Mix the speculoos and put in a bowl.
Melt the butter over low heat and add to the speculoos while mixing.
Put half of the mixture in the bottom of the verrines, strain and pour again.
In a saucepan, put 3 peeled and chopped peaches, add the sugar little by little.
Once cooked, mash them with a fork.
Spread the compote on the bottom then add the other half of the mixture.
For the mousse:
Bring the milk to a boil with a teaspoon of vanilla flavoring.
Beat the egg yolks with 60 g of sugar, the mixture should be
frothy, add the cornstarch, mixing well.
Pour the hot milk into the egg yolk/sugar/maïzena, then put back on the
fire, stirring well, until the mixture thickens, let it cool.
Beat egg whites until stiff with remaining sugar.
Add the stiffly beaten egg whites gently to the mixture with a marquise.
Put in the fridge for at least two hours.

Chocolate, raisin and pine nut cookies
cookies: 30

Preparation time: 15 min

Ingredients

200g sugar
125g melted butter
250g of flour
100g of chocolate
100g of pine nuts
1 handful of raisins
1 small glass of orange blossom
Rumbrun
1 packet of baking powder
1 pinch of salt

Preparation

Preheat your oven to 170°C.
Leave the butter outside to cool. If you are in a hurry you can microwave it in a
bowl for 10 to 20 seconds. Be careful the butter should not be liquid.
In a small cup, put a handful of raisins and cover with rum at the same level. Microwave
for about 20 seconds and let the raisins soak up the rum while you prepare the rest.
From time to time, stir the raisins so that they are all well saturated with rum.
In a mixing bowl, combine the flour, baking powder and a pinch of salt.

In a second bowl, firmly beat the egg, add the softened butter, sugar
and orange blossom. Mix everything energetically.
Pour the previous egg/sugar mixture over the flour. Add the chocolate chips and pine nuts and
mix to obtain a homogeneous paste. Pour in the rum/raisin mixture and finish mixing.
With the help of a tablespoon, place balls of the mixture, spaced about 3 or 4 cm apart, on a baking
sheet covered with parchment paper and bake for 8 to 10 minutes at 170°C, placing the baking
sheet in the middle of the oven. Keep an eye on them so that they are golden but not overcooked.
Let cool for 5 minutes before eating. You will get tasty cookies:
crispy on the outside and soft on the inside.

Raisin cookies
Pieces: 15

Preparation time: 15 min

Ingredients

200g sugar
250g of flour
1 packet of baking powder
4 eggs
25cl of oil
1 pinch of salt
1 handful of raisins

Preparation

Preheat the oven to 200°C (thermostat 6/7).
Mix flour, sugar and baking powder.
Add oil and eggs one by one.
Add the raisins (with rum it's even better).
Pour the dough into small dishes and bake for 15 minutes at 200°C (thermostat 6/7).

Express cakes with almonds and Nutella
pieces: 12

Preparation time: 10 min

Ingredients

200g of sugar
2 eggs
60g melted butter
20cl of fresh cream
2 teaspoons almonds
150g of flour
1/2 sachet of baking powder
12 teaspoons of nutella

Preparation

Mix the ingredients in order, except the Nutella, to form a dough.
Put a layer of dough in muffin type moulds, a good teaspoon
of Nutella, then another layer of dough.
Bake for 15 minutes at 180°C (gas mark 6).

Muffins apple, banana, chocolate...
muffins: 35

Preparation time: 20 min

Ingredients

200g of sugar
3 eggs
1 sachet of yeast
450g of flour
210g of semi-salted butter
Rum (optional)
1 apple
1 banana
1 chocolate bar (200g)
Cinnamon

Preparation

Beat the eggs and sugar together.
Once the mixture is homogeneous, add the melted butter.
Add the sifted yeast and the flour.
Mix well until you get a smooth dough.
Pour in 2 capfuls of rum for flavoring.
Divide the dough into 3 equal portions.
Cut the apple into very small pieces. Add them to the first third of the dough
with a good dose of cinnamon (depending on your taste).
Cut the banana into small pieces.
Take 1/3 of the chocolate bar and, using a knife, cut it into
chips. Add to the second third of the dough.
Take 1/3 of the chocolate bar and melt it with a little butter. Mix the melted
chocolate with the remaining dough. Make nuggets with the last part of
the bar and integrate them into the third third of the dough.
Place in hot oven in muffin tins.
As with all cakes, check with the tip of a knife during baking to ensure the consistency you want.

Cupcake base
Serves: 10

Preparation time: 1 hour

Ingredients

200g powdered sugar
110g of butter
2 eggs
200g of flour
1/2 sachet of baking powder
2 teaspoons vanilla liquid
12cl of milk
2 tablespoons cocoa powder

Preparation

Cream the butter and sugar together.
Add the eggs one by one, then add the vanilla.
Mix the yeast and the flour and incorporate them in two times, do the same with the milk.
Mix the cocoa with water until you get a paste. Add this mixture to
half of the preparation to make chocolate cupcakes.
Fill each cupcake 3/4 full. Bake for 20 to 25 minutes at 180°C (gas mark 6).

Anna cake (tender apple and pear cake)
Serves 6

Preparation time: 10 min

Ingredients

200g powdered sugar
200g of flour
4 eggs
60g of butter
1 pack of yeast
2 tablespoons of water
1 pinch of salt
4 apples or 4 pears (or 2 of each!)

Preparation

Beat together the flour, yeast, sugar and whole eggs in a bowl.
Add salt and water to make a coarse dough.
Melt the butter and add to the batter.
Cut peeled fruit into thin wedges.
Pour half of the batter into a buttered and floured baking pan.
Add the fruit slices in the shape of a rosette for example (don't hesitate to push
them in a little). Then add the rest of the dough and any leftover fruit.
Bake in a preheated oven at thermostat 5-6 (165°C) depending on the oven, for 20 to 25 min.
Enjoy!

Vanilla macaroons

pieces approx.: 40

Preparation time: 2 h

Ingredients

200g powdered sugar
200g almond powder
120g of egg white
8cl of water
200g powdered sugar
1 red color (or other color)

Preparation

For this recipe, a food brush is necessary.
For the shells:
In a bowl, beat the egg whites until stiff. Set aside.
Bring water and powdered sugar to a boil until it reaches 118°C. Remove from heat.
While beating, pour the syrup over the egg whites for 5 minutes, the meringue should be shiny.
Add the chosen coloring until the desired color is obtained.
Sift the almond powder and powdered sugar. Add one third of this mixture
to the meringue with a spatula, taking care to gently fold in.
Once the first part is properly mixed, add the rest and mix in the same way.
Your pastry shell is ready.
Preheat the oven to 150°C (gas mark 5).
Fill a piping bag with the dough, then form rounds of about 3 to 4 cm in diameter.
Let stand for 10 minutes, then bake for 12 minutes at 150°C (gas mark 5).
For the filling:
Bring the milk to a boil with the two open vanilla beans.
Meanwhile, mix the sugar and cornstarch, whisking vigorously
to avoid lumps, add the egg and mix.
Once the milk is boiling, remove the two pods and add to the egg, sugar and cornstarch mixture.
Return to the heat and add half the butter, stirring constantly until the mixture thickens.
Remove from heat and let cool.
Once the mixture has cooled, add the remaining tempered butter to the
cream, beating it with a whisk until it forms a mousseline.
Put the cream in a piping bag and garnish the macaroons generously.
For decoration, apply the golden powder with a wet brush.
You are free to choose your own designs!

Macaroons with coffee of grandma

macaroons: 40

Preparation time: 1 h

Ingredients

200g of powdered sugar
200g almond powder
160g of egg white
Liquid coffee extract
200g of caster sugar

Preparation

The macaroons :
Roast the almond powder for about 10 minutes in the oven at 150°C (thermostat 5). Let it cool and then sift the almond powder with the powdered sugar.
Beat the egg whites with half the caster sugar at a speed of 3 (medium), but not faster. This step is long and takes about 12 minutes. When the whites are stiff, leave the mixer running and add the other half of the caster sugar. Beat for another 3 minutes. The whites should be firm and form a bird's beak on the whisk.
Add the tant pour tant (mixture of almond powder and powdered sugar) to the whites and start stirring with a maryse (flat spatula) starting from the bottom and in a circle, then folding the mixture on top. When the mixture is homogeneous, add the coffee extract and stir again without hesitation.
When the dough is smooth and shiny, use a piping bag to form macaroons of about the same size (about 3 to 4 cm in diameter) on a sheet of parchment paper stuck with a little dough on an ovenproof baking sheet.
Put in the oven for about 12 minutes at 160°C (gas mark 5-6) and keep an eye on the cooking time, as the macaroons should not colour. Allow to cool before removing.
For the ganache :
Cut the chocolate into small pieces.
Heat the cream with the soluble coffee and bring to a boil.
Pour the cream over the chocolate and stir until the chocolate is completely melted and the mixture is smooth. Allow to cool to room temperature then place in the refrigerator for at least 1 hour.
Using a piping bag, fill half of the shells and close by turning to spread the ganache.
Place the macaroons in an airtight box and refrigerate for about 12 hours.

Melting chocolate muffins
pieces: 8

Preparation time: 20 min

Ingredients

200g of brown sugar
1 sachet of vanilla sugar
100g of flour
70g of sweetened cocoa powder
5g of yeast
2 eggs
100g of soft butter
1 tablespoon of milk

Preparation

Mix the brown sugar, vanilla sugar, flour (sifted is better!), cocoa powder
and yeast in a bowl until the mixture is smooth.
Put the butter in a bowl and melt it in the microwave. Then mix it with the contents of the bowl.
Add 1 tablespoon of milk and mix again.
Separate the egg yolks and egg whites: put the yolks in the bowl and mix.
Beat your egg whites until stiff. Fold the egg whites into the bowl, mixing in an airy manner.
The batter is ready! Take your muffin tins and fill them about 3/4 full of batter.
Then, put them in the oven halfway up for about 15 minutes at 200°C
(thermostat 6-7). The knife should come out slightly moist.
To be eaten warm after baking for the fondant side, or cooled for a chocolate explosion!

Small cakes with raspberry

cakes: 20

Preparation time: 10 min

Ingredients

200g brown sugar
200g of flour
200g of butter
1 sachet of baking powder
4 eggs
1pod of raspberries
1 teaspoon lemon (if you like)
Whipped cream (optional)

Preparation

Put the soft butter in the bowl of a mixer after having cut it in small
pieces. Add the sugar and whiten the mixture.
Gradually add the flour, then the eggs one by one, and finally the packet of baking
powder. Don't forget the teaspoon of lemon extract if you like a more acidic taste.
Spoon a tablespoon of the dough into the 20 floured paper ramekins. Sprinkle
with the rinsed raspberries.
Put another 2 tablespoons of dough into the ramekins and bake for 20
minutes at gas mark 5 (165°C) in a preheated oven.
Let the cakes cool and garnish with a little whipped cream if you wish.

Milk chocolate chip cookies

Serves: 25

Preparation time: 20 min

Ingredients

200g brown sugar

350g of flour
2 eggs
200g of butter
1 sachet of vanilla sugar
1 sachet of yeast
1 pinch of salt
1 bar of milk chocolate (170 g) special for cooking

Preparation

Using a mixer or whisk, mix eggs and sugar for 1 minute.
Add flour, salt, yeast and butter.
Knead the dough by hand.
Crush the chocolate bar and insert the pieces into the dough.
Preheat oven to 200°C (gas mark 6-7) for 15 minutes.
Place the dough balls sufficiently spaced out (about 7 per plate).
Bake for 10 minutes.
When removed, place on a wire rack and let cool so that the cookies take on their final consistency.

Orange zest tuiles without butter
about 50 pieces

Preparation time: 10 min

Ingredients

200g caster sugar
200g of fresh cream
150g of flour
100g of flaked almonds
orange peel

Preparation

Beat the cream and the sugar. Gradually add the flour and almonds.
Take the orange peel and grate it finely. Pour all the zest into the
dough with 1 tablespoon of orange juice.
Spoon the dough into small tiles on a baking sheet covered with parchment paper.
Bake for 5 minutes at 180°C (gas mark 6).
Remove the cooked slices with a knife and place them on a bottle or rolling pin to form tiles.

Marbled cookie covered with chocolate
Serves 6

Preparation time: 20 min

Ingredients

200g caster sugar

8g vanilla sugar (1 sachet)
240g of butter
2 tablespoons of sweetened cocoa
1 teaspoon of baking powder
3 eggs
200g flour
100g chocolate for the icing
1 cake tin

Preparation

Preheat your oven to 180°C (thermostat 6).
In a bowl, beat the melted butter with the caster sugar until the mixture turns white. Incorporate the egg yolks while continuing to beat. Sift the flour with the yeast and add to the mixture, mixing well to obtain a smooth dough.
Beat the egg whites until stiff, then gently fold them into the mixture, stirring until a smooth paste is obtained.
Separate the dough into 2 separate containers. Add the vanilla sugar to one and the cocoa to the other. You will obtain 2 doughs of 2 colors.
In a buttered cake pan, alternate layers of white and brown dough. Bake in a hot oven for 50 minutes.
Check the cooking with the blade of a knife and remove the marbled cookie from the pan onto a wire rack.
While it is cooling, prepare the glaze by melting the chocolate with 2 tablespoons of water.
Using a spatula, spread the melted chocolate over the cookie and let it harden.
Do not serve the marble until the topping is cold and hard.

Amaretti revisited
pieces: 20

Preparation time: 20 min

Ingredients

200 almond powder
150g of powdered sugar
2 egg whites
150g of dark chocolate
20 squares of white chocolate
125g of butter

Preparation

Preheat the oven to 160°C (thermostat 6-7).
Line a baking tray with baking paper.
In a bowl, mix the almond powder, soft butter and powdered sugar.
In another bowl, beat the egg whites with a fork.
Add the almond powder, sugar and butter mixture to the bowl containing the egg whites.

Mix well.
Put in the refrigerator for at least 20 minutes.
Break your chocolate squares (20 for dark chocolate and 20 for white chocolate).
Wet your hands.
Form balls of dough the size of a large walnut.
Insert your chocolate squares inside your dough ball (two squares per ball).
Place them on the parchment paper, spacing them out and flattening them slightly.
Bake the amaretti in the oven for 17 minutes, until they are lightly
browned (they should remain soft in the middle).
Once cooled, remove from the parchment paper.
Store in a tin or enjoy.

Apricot Cookie Cake
Serves 6

Preparation time: 35 min

Ingredients

20 cookies with a spoon
4cl of rum
4cl of water
2 eggs
100g of semolina
15g of flour
75g almond powder
500g of apricots

Preparation

Preheat the oven to 180°C (gas mark 6) and butter a pie pan or a porcelain dish.
Cover the bottom and the sides of the pan with the cookies with a spoon. Arrange
them vertically and cut them so that they protrude a little from the edge.
Prepare a mixture of rum and water and dip the cookies in it.
Prepare an almond cream:
Whisk the egg yolks with the sugar until the mixture foams and turns white. Add flour
and almond powder. Whip the egg whites until stiff and fold in with a spatula.
Pour the mixture over the cookies. Cut the apricots in half and place the
halves on the cream. Press them lightly into the mixture.
Bake for 40 minutes.
Serve warm or cold.

No-bake chocolate cookie
Serves 6

Preparation time: 20 min

Ingredients

20 small butter cookies
100g of flaked almonds
1brick of condensed milk
200g of dark chocolate

Preparation

Crumble the biscuits into a large bowl.
Melt the chocolate.
Add 100g of flaked almonds, condensed milk and melted chocolate.
Mix well.
Pour the preparation into muffin tins.
Leave to cool for 2 to 3 hours.
Turn out the cookies and cover with melted chocolate.

Tiramisu with pears and speculoos
Serves 8

Preparation time: 30 min

Ingredients

20 speculoos cookies
250g of mascarpone
5 eggs
1 pinch of salt (for the egg whites)
80sugar
1 sachet vanilla sugar
2 juicy pears

Preparation

Separate the whites from the yolks. Blanch the egg yolks with
the sugar, then add the mascarpone. Set aside.
Wash, peel and seed the pears. Cover the bottom of a gratin dish with speculoos,
then with a layer of pears cut into slices about 2 mm thick. The cookies will drink the
juice of the pears which will replace the coffee of the traditional tiramisus.
Beat the egg whites until stiff. Gently fold them into the yolk mixture. Spread this mixture in
the dish and place in the refrigerator for 4 hours. Sprinkle sparingly with cinnamon powder.

Milk Cream Cookies or Claque
cookies: 18

Preparation time: 20 min

Ingredients

20cl of cream
1 pinch of salt

20g of powdered sugar
100g of flour

Preparation

Preheat the oven to 8 on a scale of 10, as for a pie.
Put the cream, salt and sugar in a bowl, mix, add flour until the mixture
is thick but still too sticky to knead by hand.
With two small spoons, place small packages of dough the size of a walnut
on a non-stick baking sheet.
Bake for about 10 minutes in a hot oven, the cookies should remain golden.

Cookie with almonds au gratin
Serves 6

Preparation time: 15 min

Ingredients

20cl of heavy cream
2pots of fine sugar (320g approximately)
1 jar of flour (80 g approx.)
4 eggs
1 packet of yeast
1 packet of vanilla sugar
125g melted butter
4 tablespoons of milk
125g of almonds

Preparation

Preheat your oven to 210°C (thermostat 7).
Mix the cream with the sugar, eggs, vanilla sugar, flour and baking powder.
Spread the dough in a thin layer on a baking sheet or a large flat pan. Bake for 10 minutes.
Mix together the rest of the ingredients (milk, almonds, the 2nd jar of
sugar, butter) and spread the preparation on the cake.
Bake for a few minutes under the broiler.

All chocolate macadamia nut cookie
Serves 8

Preparation time: 20 min

Ingredients

20cl of liquid cream
1egg
1 teaspoon of vanilla extract
275g caster sugar

150g of flour
1/2 sachet of yeast
1/2 teaspoon of bicarbonate
35g of cocoa
150g of dark chocolate
Milk
100g of macadamia nuts

Preparation

Preheat the oven to 180°C (thermostat 6).
Quickly whip the cream, vanilla extract, sugar and egg. Then add
the flour, baking powder, baking soda and cocoa.
Finally, add the chocolate chips and macadamia nuts previously cut.
On a baking sheet covered with baking paper, place small piles of dough at regular
intervals and bake for 15 minutes. Let the cookies rest for at least 5 minutes before
removing them from the baking paper. Then let them cool on a flat surface.

Small flans apple palet breton heart nutella
people: 4

Preparation time: 10 min

Ingredients

20cl of liquid cream
20cl of milk
1 sachet of vanilla sugar
40g of powdered sugar
1 golden apple
4 teaspoons of nutella
3 eggs

Preparation

Peel the apple and cut it into thin wedges.
Mix the eggs with the sugar and vanilla sugar, add the milk and the cream, place
the apple quarters in the bottom of a small casserole dish, place the Breton puck
in the bottom and gently pour the mixture over it, add a spoonful of nutella
in the middle, and bake for 25 minutes at 180°C (thermostat 6).

Easy oatmeal cookies
Serves 10

Preparation time: 5 min

Ingredients

20cl of oatmeal

1 glass of coconut milk
1 cup of flour
1gallon sugar (optional, half brown, half white)
1/2 cup of finely chopped hazelnuts
200g margarine
2 tablespoons honey
1 teaspoon vanilla liquid

Preparation

Preheat the oven to 200°C (gas mark 6-7).
Mix all the dry ingredients in a large bowl: oatmeal, coconut, flour, sugar and hazelnuts.
Melt the margarine, honey and vanilla in the microwave and mix with the dry product mixture.
Place a sheet of parchment paper on a large flat baking pan.
Pour in the batter (not liquid at all), and (not liquid at all), and press down well.
Put in the oven for exactly 6 minutes (you need a timer here!).
Remove from the oven and cut into squares using the pizza cutter.
Return to the oven for 1 min.
Wait until completely cooled to separate the cookies.
DELICIOUS AND VERY VERY EASY!

Very light chocolate coconut muffins
muffins: 20

Preparation time: 20 min

Ingredients

20cl of coconut milk
50g butter
100g of flour
50g of starch
75g of sugar
1 sachet of vanilla sugar
1 sachet of baking powder
2 eggs
110g of grated coconut
150g of chocolate

Preparation

Melt the butter.
Add the coconut milk and mix well.
Add sugar, flour, cornstarch and yeast.
Separate the white from the yolks. Add the yolks to the previous mixture.
Beat the whites until they are stiff. Then incorporate them delicately into the mixture.
Add the coconut and chocolate chips! Mix well!
Pour the batter into muffin tins (silicone for me). Put in a hot oven
for about 15 minutes at 180°C (thermostat 6).

Cocoa Tuiles
Serves 6

Preparation time: 15 min

Ingredients

20g of cocoa
20g of flour
30g of milk
25g of honey
25g of butter
15cl of orange juice

Preparation

Melt the butter, add the honey, the flour, the milk powder, the cocoa and pour the orange juice.
Leave to rest for 1 hour and spread on a buttered tray.
Bake in medium oven (150°C) for 5 minutes.
Remove the tiles with a spatula and mould them on a rolling pin.

Honey almond shortbread
Cookies: 20

Preparation time: 15 min

Ingredients

20g of sugar
60g of butter
1 egg
150g of flour
40g almond powder
50g of liquid honey

Preparation

Melt the butter. Preheat the oven to 180°C (thermostat 6).
In the bowl, introduce the flour, sugar, egg and butter and mix by hand.
Then add the almond powder and the honey according to your taste.
Knead the dough and then make balls the size of a walnut that you
will place on the grid or the plate of your oven.
Bake for 15 to 20 minutes in your oven at 180°C, it's ready!

Christmas cookies with hazelnuts (Nüsskipfel)
cookies: 40

Preparation time: 10 min

Ingredients

210g butter
250g flour
200g hazelnut powder
170g of sugar
1 sachet of vanilla sugar
6 tablespoons of powdered sugar

Preparation

Mix the butter, flour and hazelnut powder to obtain a dough.
Roll it into a sausage of about 2.5 cm in diameter.
Put in the fridge for 1 hour.
Cut into slices of 1 to 2 cm thick, and form into croissants (shape like Croissants de lune).
Bake at 175°C (thermostat 5-6) for about 15 minutes.
Let cool for a few moments, before rolling them in a mixture of powdered sugar and vanilla sugar (be careful: the cookies are crumbly when they come out of the oven!).
Store in a cool, dry place.

Low-fat chocolate chip muffins
muffins: 12

Preparation time: 10 min

Ingredients

210g flour
150g sugar
2 teaspoons of yeast
25cl of skimmed milk
60g of low-fat butter
100g of chocolate
1/2 teaspoon of vanilla

Preparation

Preheat the oven to 180°C (thermostat 6).
Mix the flour, yeast and sugar.
In a separate bowl, mix the melted butter, milk and vanilla.
Make a hole in the flour and pour in the milk and butter.
Mix, but not too much, there must be some lumps left for it to swell up!
Stir in the sprinkles.
Butter 12 muffin tins or use silicone moulds.
Fill them 3/4 of the way and bake for about 20 minutes.
Enjoy!

Cocoa-chocolate macaroons
pieces: 40

Preparation time :

Ingredients

210g powdered sugar
50g of coconut powder
60g almond powder
4 egg whites
200g cooking chocolate
20cl coconut milk or cream

Preparation

Beat the egg whites for 5 to 10 minutes to obtain a block, adding a little sugar at the same time.
In another bowl, mix the powdered sugar, almond powder and coconut powder.
With a spatula add the egg whites gradually. Mix everything together.
Place small piles of dough on baking paper.
Cook for 12 to 15 minutes at 180°C (gas mark 6).
Prepare the ganache by melting the chocolate in a bain-marie with the coconut milk.
To assemble, place a teaspoon of ganache in one shell and cover with a second.
Repeat the operation.

Mascarpone fruit compote muffins
muffins: 9

Preparation time: 20 min

Ingredients

220g farina (whole wheat if desired)
2 tablespoons baking powder
1 teaspoon of bicarbonate
90g of brown sugar
1 egg
½ basket of strawberries
½ papaya
almonds
2 spoons of mascarpone
1 spoonful of maple butter or butter

Preparation

Cut the strawberries and half a papaya into pieces. Cook them with the sugar until
you get a compote. Melt the mascarpone and butter (maple), add the almond essence.
With a blender, coarsely reduce the compote (leave some pieces, it's good too).
In a bowl, add the flour, baking powder, baking soda and egg. Add the compote
and mix well to obtain a soft dough.
Line the muffin tin with paper trays and fill the trays with the batter.
Bake at 220°C in a preheated oven for 20 minutes.

Almond and pineapple muffins
muffins: 12

Preparation time: 15 min

Ingredients

220g almond powder
220g sugar
1dl of water
4 eggs
100g of butter
55g of flour
1/2 sachet of yeast

Preparation

In a bowl, knead the almond powder with the sugar and water.
Add the eggs one by one, then the melted butter, flour and yeast.
Let the dough rest for 1 hour in the refrigerator.
Place in the muffin cups. Place a few pieces of pineapple (or apple, pear or apricot) on each one.
Bake for about 10 minutes in a preheated oven at 240°C (th 8).
Let cool before serving.

Delicious American salted butter cookies
cookies: 20

Preparation time: 20 min

Ingredients

220g flour
1/2 packet of baking powder
50g brown sugar
50g of white sugar
1 sachet of vanilla sugar
125g of salted butter
1 teaspoon of honey
1 egg
60g of chocolate
Caramel to your taste

Preparation

Preheat your oven to 200°C (thermostat 6-7).
In a bowl, melt the butter in the microwave (wait for it to cool)
and mix it with the honey and the egg.
In another container, mix flour, baking powder and sugars (vanilla, brown sugar and white).

Bring everything together and mix (the dough is lumpy, that's normal)
then add the chocolate chips and caramel chips.
On your baking sheet, put baking paper and form small balls of
dough and space them well (cook in 2 batches).
Put in the oven at 200°C (thermostat 6-7) for about 5 to 8 minutes,
keep an eye on them, let them cool and enjoy!

Cookies with nuts
cookies: 30

Preparation time: 30 min

Ingredients

220g of flour
100g of butter
100g of sugar
1 egg
2 spoons of yogurt
1 sachet of yeast
1 pinch of salt
50g of nuts

Preparation

Preheat the oven to 180°C.
Melt the butter.
Add sugar, egg, yogurt and salt.
Mix. Then add the flour and the yeast.
Shape the cookies into 10 cm pieces and place a walnut kernel on each cookie.
Bake for about 20 minutes.

Christmas shortbread with almond powder
Serves 6

Preparation time: 20 min

Ingredients

220g of flour
100g of butter
100g of powdered sugar
70g almond powder
1 egg yolk
1 egg yolk
1 teaspoon of yeast
Cinnamon
Nutmeg

Preparation

Preheat the oven to 200°C (thermostat 6-7).
In a bowl, mix the flour with the yeast, sugar and almond powder.
Break the egg and add the softened butter. Start to mix the preparation with a fork then knead the dough with the hand to incorporate the butter well.
Add the cinnamon and nutmeg and work the dough again for a few minutes.
Using a rolling pin, roll out the dough on a floured work surface.
Then cut out the cookies with a cookie cutter.
Arrange the shortbread on a parchment-lined baking sheet.
Brush the top of the shortbread with the egg yolk to obtain a nice golden color.
Place in the oven for 8 to 10 minutes (to be watched).
Let the cookies cool before eating.

Simple and delicious cookies
pieces: 25

Preparation time: 15 min

Ingredients

220g flour
100g of butter
100g of white sugar
100g brown sugar
100g baking chocolate
1 egg
1/2 teaspoon baking soda
1 pinch of salt

Preparation

Chop the chocolate coarsely, and mix the soft butter with the two sugars and the egg.
Add the flour, the bicarbonate, the salt and finally the chocolate.
Work the dough by hand.
Make balls and place them on a baking sheet covered with parchment paper.
Bake in the preheated oven at 180°C (gas mark 6) for about 15 minutes.

Apricot shortbread cake
Serves 8

Preparation time: 25 min

Ingredients

220g of flour
10g brown sugar or sugar
75g oil

75g of butter
1 egg
5g of baker's yeast
10cl of milk
Salt

Preparation

Preheat the oven to 180°C (thermostat 6).
Prepare the dough by placing the flour in a bowl and adding the sugar and
salt. Mix. Melt the butter and dissolve the yeast in the warm milk.
Add the milk + yeast mixture to the flour, as well as the melted butter, oil and finally the
egg. Mix well, the dough should have a nice sandy consistency. Let it rest for two hours.
Meanwhile, prepare the filling: wash the apricots, remove the stones and cut them in
half. Place the flour, sugar, almond powder and butter in a bowl and mix well.
After two hours, when the dough has rested well, roll it out with a rolling
pin, butter a cake tin and place the dough in it.
Place the apricots on the dough and cover entirely with the sandy almond mixture.
Bake for 45 minutes. Serve warm or cold.

Rhubarb Banana Muffins
Small muffins: 15

Preparation time: 15 min

Ingredients

220g of flour
130g sugar
2 teaspoons of baking powder
1 teaspoon of salt
1 pinch of cinnamon
1 egg
5cl of oil
2 ripe bananas
180g of diced rhubarb

Preparation

In a first bowl, mix the dry ingredients: flour, sugar, yeast, salt and cinnamon.
In a second bowl, whisk together the egg, oil and mashed bananas.
Quickly mix the two preparations and add the rhubarb.
Just reduce the lumps and don't try to get a smooth batter (that's the secret of puffy muffins!).
Immediately pour into a buttered and floured muffin tin.
Bake for 20 to 25 minutes at 180°C (gas mark 6).

Pistachio and white chocolate cookies
large cookies: 15

Preparation time: 20 min

Ingredients

220g of flour
200g white chocolate
110g of butter
160g of sugar
2 tablespoons of caster sugar
1 egg
1 teaspoon of yeast
1/2 teaspoon of pistachios
1 drop of green coloring

Preparation

Cut the white chocolate bar into chips. Preheat the oven to 140°C (gas mark 5).
Mix the softened butter with the 2 sugars with an electric mixer. The
dough should thicken, turn white and become sticky.
Incorporate the egg, then the flour, the yeast and finish with the pistachio extract
and the coloring. Mix well. Then add the white chocolate chips.
Place parchment paper on a baking sheet.
Make piles of cookie dough, spacing them well apart (they will
spread and double in size during baking).
Bake for 10 to 15 minutes depending on your taste (if you like them more or less cooked).

Chocolate, lemon, honey and ginger muffin
Serves 6

Preparation time: 35 min

Ingredients

220g of flour
40g of brown sugar
30cl of milk
2 teaspoons of baking powder
1 teaspoon of bicarbonate
1 pinch of salt
2 eggs
75g of butter
1 packet of vanilla sugar
4 squares of chocolate lemon ginger
1 tablespoon of caramel
2 tablespoons of bee's honey
jar of spread

Preparation

Preheat the oven to 180°C (gas mark 6).
Take two bowls.
In the first one put: flour, sugar, salt, bicarbonate, baking powder, vanilla sugar.
Mix well.
In a saucepan melt the honey, chocolate, liquid caramel with a little
milk. (Can be melted in the microwave).
In the second bowl put: the beaten eggs, the softened butter, and the melted mixture previously.
Mix well.
In the first dish make a well.
Add the second mixture.
Mix quickly so that it is homogeneous.
Do not beat the mixture too long, the dough should be lumpy.
Place the dough in ramekins or muffin tins.
Fill them 1/4 full. Add a dab of Nutella (optional). Finish filling to 3/4.
Place in the oven at 180°C (gas mark 6) for 20 minutes.
Serve slightly warm.

Honey muffins
muffins: 7

Preparation time: 15 min

Ingredients

220g flour
55g brown sugar
2 teaspoons baking powder
1 teaspoon of bicarbonate
1/2 teaspoon of salt
2 beaten eggs
125ml liquid honey
125ml orange juice
75g butter
1 teaspoon vanilla extract

Preparation

Preheat the oven to 190°C and butter the muffin tins.
Mix the following ingredients in two separate containers:
Mix 1: flour, yeast, salt, sugar, bicarbonate.
Mix 2: eggs, honey, orange juice, butter and vanilla.
Make a well in mixture 1 and add mixture 2.
Mix lightly and quickly, but do not overbeat the dough, it should look lumpy.
Using a tablespoon, fill the molds with dough to 2 / 3 and bake 15 to 20 minutes.
Leave to cool and then turn out onto a wire rack.

White chocolate, speculoos and coconut cookies

Cookies: 25

Preparation time: 20 min

Ingredients

220g flour
60g sugar (brown or white)
2 packets of vanilla sugar
100g of butter
2 eggs
1 sachet of baking powder
1 pinch of salt
150g of white chocolate
50g of grated coconut
60g of speculoos (about 6 cookies)
2 tablespoons of rum

Preparation

Preheat your oven to 170°C (thermostat 5-6).
Cut the chocolate into cubes (more or less large for a more or less greedy effect).
Place the speculoos in a shallow dish and crumble them finely or coarsely according
to your preference. (With a glass bottom for example).
Mix the butter, sugar and vanilla sugar until the mixture turns white.
Add the eggs, then the flour, salt, baking powder and finally the rum. Mix vigorously!
Now you can add the white chocolate and speculoos crumbs, as
well as the grated coconut. Spread them evenly!
Now it's time to shape your cookies: using two tablespoons, an ice cream
scoop, or your hands, create small balls of varying sizes.
Don't forget to space them out enough because the cookies spread out a bit when they are cooked.
Bake them at 170°C (thermostat 5-6) for 12 to 15 minutes.
Let them cool on a rack and enjoy!

Banana and walnut muffins
mini muffins: 12

Preparation time: 10 min

Ingredients

220g wholemeal flour
120g of butter
1 packet of baking powder
2 eggs
130g of sugar
3 ripe bananas
100g walnut kernel
200ml whole milk

1 teaspoon of allspice

Preparation

Preheat the oven to thermostat 6 (180°C).
Cut the bananas in small quarters.
Brown them in 20 g of butter. Sprinkle with sugar. Set aside.
Mix the rest of the butter with the sugar, until the mixture becomes homogeneous.
Add the eggs and milk.
Mix the flour with the yeast, sifting it so that it becomes homogeneous.
Incorporate the flour into the mixture.
Add the spices, the chopped or whole nuts, and finally the bananas.
Mix but do not overwork the batter.
Put in a muffin tin... If it's a rigid pan, grease it first, but if it's a silicone
pan, pour the mixture directly into it.
Bake at thermostat 6 (180°C) for 30 minutes.
Once cooked, the muffins should be removed from the pan immediately and put on a plate to cool.
Bon appétit!

Raspberry and chocolate muffins
muffins: 12

Preparation time: 10 min

Ingredients

220g frozen raspberries
160g dark chocolate
80g of oatmeal
1/2 sachet of baking powder

Preparation

Keep about 15 raspberries in a cool place and mix all the others together.
Melt the chocolate in the microwave (in several steps) or in a double boiler.
Add the chocolate to the previous mixture and blend again.
Pour the mixture into a bowl and add the oats and yeast. Mix well.
Pour into muffin tins and push in the whole raspberries that we had kept in the center of each cake.
Bake for 18 minutes at 180°C, remove and let cool before unmolding.

Trio of Nutella® mini-muffins
Serves 4

Preparation time: 13 min

Ingredients

220g of sugar
4 eggs
264g of flour

60g of butter
60ml sunflower oil
180g cornstarch
1 sachet of baking powder
4g of salt
80g of mashed potatoes
80g carrot purée

Preparation

Mix the eggs and the sugar in a mixer, add the dry ingredients and finally the oil and the butter.
Divide the resulting mixture into three equal parts. In a second bowl, add
the mashed carrots to another third of the dough - In a third bowl, add
60 g of crushed hazelnuts to the last third of the dough.
Fill mini-muffin tins with the three preparations (20-25 grams of dough per tin).
Bake for 15 minutes at 180°C (gas mark 6).
Before serving, decorate each muffin with 15 g of Nutella® and some crushed hazelnuts.

Hazelnut cookies
Serves 4

Preparation time: 10 min

Ingredients

225g soft butter
180g of caster sugar
2 eggs
225g of flour
70g hazelnut chips
2 teaspoons vanilla liquid

Preparation

Beat together butter, sugar and eggs.
Mix the flour and hazelnut chips together. Then add to the previous mixture.
Add the vanilla.
Place by large teaspoonfuls on a non-stick baking sheet.
Bake at 180°C for 12-15 minutes (until lightly browned).
Remove from pan immediately, place on a wire rack.

Peanut butter cookies
cookies: 20

Preparation time: 20 min

Ingredients

225g butter, softened

200g white sugar
220g brown sugar
2 eggs
1 egg yolk
10ml vanilla liquid
455g peanut butter
250g of flour
5g of yeast
3g of salt

Preparation

In a large bowl, mix butter, white sugar and brown sugar until smooth.
Add eggs, yolks and vanilla; mix until fluffy.
Sift together flour, baking powder and salt; add to peanut butter and mix.
Refrigerate the dough for at least 2 hours.
Preheat the oven to 175°C.
Lightly grease the baking sheet.
Make small balls. Place them on the prepared baking sheet and flatten slightly with a fork.
Bake for 12 to 15 minutes in the preheated oven.
The cookies should look dry on top.
Let cool and enjoy.

Gluten free chocolate chip cookies
pieces: 27

Preparation time: 15 min

Ingredients

225g butter at temperature
375g glutinous rice flour
2 bags of chocolate (about 200 grams)
2 eggs
150g caster sugar
150g brown sugar
1 teaspoon vanilla extract
1 pinch of salt
2 teaspoons of bicarbonate

Preparation

Before starting the recipe, put your nugget bags in a freezer drawer and preheat the oven to 190°C. Mix the flour with the baking soda and the pinch of salt in a bowl.
In a food processor or a bowl if you have elbow grease to spare, put the butter (at room temperature, i.e. quite soft, almost oily), the caster and brown sugar and start mixing. When the mixture is homogeneous, add the eggs one by one while mixing, then the vanilla extract.
Add the flour-bicarbonate-salt mixture gradually to the previous mixture while mixing.

If you used a food processor, transfer the mixture to a bowl. Take the bags out of the freezer and add them to the mixture. Chilling them before using them prevents them from melting in the machine if it is too hot.
Little tip: to form the dough balls (preferably on a silicone plate), use an ice cream scoop (the one with a spring) and you will have cookies of the same size. Bake them for 20 minutes at 190°C.
When they come out of the oven the cookies are quite crumbly due to the rice flour, but don't worry they will harden as they cool, so leave them alone.

Spiced shortbread
Serves 8

Preparation time: 15 min

Ingredients

225g butter
175g of cane sugar
1 egg white
2 teaspoons of cinnamon
1 teaspoon of ginger
1 large pinch of salt
275g of flour

Preparation

Crush the butter and make it soft. Add the sugar and stir to obtain a light mixture.
Add the egg white, cinnamon, ginger and salt. Beat until the mixture is creamy.
Finally, gradually add the flour.
Roll out the dough on floured baking sheets or parchment paper, or baking sheets until you have a very thin layer (the delicate part of the recipe). Use the number of baking sheets needed depending on the size and thickness of your rolled out dough.
Bake at 180-190°C (gas mark 6-7) for 15 minutes until the dough is pale and a little puffy.
Watch the first time as it may cook faster.
Remove the baking sheets from the oven and cut the dough into diamonds, let cool completely.
Ideal to freeze: put the cookies in a special freezer box, close and freeze.
To defrost: leave 10 to 15 minutes at room temperature.
You can play with the spices by removing the cinnamon, increasing the ginger, adding vanilla.

Kangoo shortbread
Serves 6

Preparation time: 20 min

Ingredients

225g of butter
210g of powdered sugar
1 egg

1 teaspoon of vanilla extract
350g of flour
2 teaspoons of yeast
1 pinch of salt
200g of chocolate

Preparation

Preheat the oven to 200°C (thermostat 6-7).
Separately, beat the egg with the vanilla and add to the previous preparation.
Mix well until you obtain a homogeneous preparation.
Add flour, baking powder and salt. Mix well.
Work the dough with your hands if necessary, it should not be sticky, add flour
if necessary.Wrap the dough in cling film and keep in a cool place.
Roll out the dough on a floured work surface to a thickness of 1/2 to 1 cm.
Cut out rectangles of dough, place 2 squares of chocolate in the
center of each rectangle and fold over the edges.
Place on a baking sheet covered with baking paper and bake for 12 minutes.

Mom's shortbread

Serves 6

Preparation time: 10 min

Ingredients

225g of butter
225g of sugar
2 eggs
1 teaspoon of vanilla
2 teaspoons baking powder
500g of flour

Preparation

In a bowl, mix the butter, sugar, eggs, vanilla and baking powder
and then add the flour in several times.
Knead the dough until you get a smooth and homogeneous consistency.
Take a small amount of dough and roll it out with a rolling pin on
a sheet of parchment paper or other surface.
With stencils, make the shapes you want.
Bake in the oven at 180°C (gas mark 6) for 10 to 15 minutes.

Easy honey shortbread

cookies: 25

Preparation time: 15 min

Ingredients

225g of flour
100g of butter
100g white or brown sugar
2 tablespoons of honey
1 egg yolk beaten
1 teaspoon of baking powder
Flavor (optional) 1 tablespoon of orange blossom or 3 drops of lemon/bergamot essential oil, etc.

Preparation

Preheat the oven to 150°C (thermostat 3)
Mix the softened butter, sugar, honey and flavouring.
Add the egg yolk and then the flour and yeast.
Form a ball and roll out on a floured plate.
And in front of the cookie cutters!
Bake the shortbread for about 15 minutes. Keep an eye on the cooking
time, it varies according to the shapes and thicknesses.
After cooling the shortbread on a rack, you can decorate it with almond
paste, sugar paste or other decorations.

Banana Sunshine Cookie
Serves: 6

Preparation time: 15 min

Ingredients

225g of flour
125g of butter
325g of sugar
2 eggs
3 bananas
3 tablespoons of milk
1 tablespoon of cinnamon
1 teaspoon vanilla powder
1 pinch of salt
1 teaspoon yeast
1 tablespoon rum (optional)

Preparation

Preheat the oven to 150°C-175°C (thermostat 5-6).
Mix the butter and the sugar.
Add the beaten eggs and mix well.
Peel and mash the bananas, add them to the mixture alternating with the flour.
Add the yeast, salt, cinnamon, vanilla, milk, and eventually the rum.
Pour into a cake pan.
Bake for about 45 minutes.

Soft Madeleines with chocolate chips and orange peel

madeleines: 32

Preparation time: 20 min

Ingredients

225g of flour
130g sugar including 14 grams of vanilla sugar
130g of soft butter
1 packet of baking powder
4 eggs
1 teaspoon of vanilla flavouring
1 pinch of salt
Chocolate
candied orange peel

Preparation

Take out the butter and let it at room temperature.
In a bowl, beat the eggs and add, in order, the sugar, vanilla sugar, salt and vanilla flavoring.
Add the sifted flour and the yeast and whisk until the mixture is completely homogeneous.
Incorporate the butter, previously worked in pomade.
Add a few chocolate chips.
Preheat oven to 230°C (gas mark 7-8).
Fill the alveoli almost to the edge and add chocolate chips and candied orange peel as desired.
Bake for 7 minutes and then continue baking for 3 minutes at
180°C (gas mark 6) until a golden shell appears.
Turn out delicately and enjoy!

Cocoa and honey muffins

large muffins: 12

Preparation time: 20 min

Ingredients

225g of flour
1 half of yeast
50g unsweetened cocoa powder
200g of semi-salted butter
150g powdered sugar
40g of honey
3 eggs

Preparation

Preheat the oven to 170°C (thermostat 5-6).
Mix the flour, yeast and cocoa in a bowl.

Mix the butter, sugar and honey in another bowl and whisk until frothy. Add the eggs
and continue to whisk. Add the flour-cocoa mixture and mix without beating.
Pour the batter into muffin tins (preferably silicone).
Bake muffins for 30 minutes.
Let cool and serve.

Lemon honey almond muffins
Serves 9

Preparation time: 40 min

Ingredients

225g of flour
1 packet of baking powder
40g of brown sugar
3 tablespoons of honey
100g of salted butter
2 eggs
2 yellow lemons
125g flaked almonds
2 tablespoons vanilla flavoring (optional)

Preparation

Preheat the oven to 240°C (gas mark 8).
Mix the eggs with the salted butter and sugar.
Add the flour and the yeast.
Finally, add the zest and juice of the 2 lemons, the honey and the almonds.
Optional: add 1 to 2 tablespoons of vanilla flavoring.
Fill the molds (no need to butter them if they are silicone) and put them
in the oven, thermostat 8 (240°C) for about 20 minutes.
Keep an eye on the cooking time from 20 min onwards (usually the
muffins are golden brown in less than 25 min).

Chocolate chip cookies (slightly shortbread)
Cookies: 20

Preparation time: 15 min

Ingredients

225g flour
225g butter
1/4 teaspoon of salt
1/2 teaspoon of baking powder
100g of powdered sugar
125g of chocolate (for me 100g is enough)

60g of chopped nuts (you can use pecans)

Preparation

Preheat your oven to 150°C (thermostat 5).
Sift the flour, baking powder and salt together and set aside.
Cream together the butter and sugar until the mixture whitens a little and becomes fluffy.
Add the butter-sugar mixture to the flour-yeast-salt mixture and mix well.
Then add the chopped nuts and chocolate chips and mix again.
Then form balls of about 4 cm in diameter and flatten them and put them on your baking paper.
Repeat the operation until there is no more dough.
Bake in the oven for 15-20 minutes, until the cookies are a little golden.

Morning glory muffins
Serves: 2

Preparation time: 15 min

Ingredients

225g flour
50g of sugar
1 packet of baking powder
1 teaspoon of cinnamon
1/2 teaspoon of salt
100g of carrots, mixed
50g of cracked nuts
50g of coconut powder
1/2 mixed apple
2 eggs
20cl of oil
1 teaspoon of vanilla

Preparation

Preheat the oven to 180°C (thermostat 6).
In a bowl, mix flour, sugar, yeast, cinnamon, salt.
Add apple, coconut, carrots, nuts and mix.
In another bowl, mix the eggs, oil and vanilla.
Finally, mix everything together and place in muffin or madeleine
molds, and bake for 20 minutes (at 180C°).

Abernethy Biscuits
cookies: 20

Preparation time: 5 min

Ingredients

225g of flour
75g butter
75g sugar (white or brown)
1 egg
50ml of milk
1/2 sachet of yeast
Vanilla sugar (optional)

Preparation

Mix flour and yeast, add butter, then sugar, working with fingertips to obtain
a crumble-like mixture.
Add the beaten egg and milk, mix well.
Flour the resulting ball of dough and roll out to about 0.5 cm thick.
Cut simple and/or funny shapes.
Bake for 12 to 15 minutes at 190°C.

Vanilla flavored chocolate pear muffins

Serves 8

Preparation time: 10 min

Ingredients

225g of pears in syrup
3 eggs
1 bag of chocolate
3 drops of vanilla extract
80g flour
80g cornstarch
125g butter
1 sachet of baking powder
120g sugar

Preparation

Preheat the oven to 180°C (thermostat 6). Melt the butter and mix it with the sugar.
Add the eggs one by one, the flour, the baking powder and a few drops of vanilla extract.
Add the pears cut into small pieces and the chocolate chips. Bake your
muffins for about 20 minutes at 180°C (thermostat 6).

The good raspberry macaroons from Monsieur Julien

macaroons: 20

Preparation time: 1h30

Ingredients

225g powdered sugar

125g almond powder
120g egg white (about 4 eggs)
60g sugar
15 drops of food coloring

Preparation

Sift the powdered sugar and powdered almonds into a bowl. Then mix with a whisk.
2) In another bowl, beat the egg whites. When the whites have set, add
the food coloring and sugar while continuing to beat.
3.incorporate this preparation with the first one. Do not hesitate to break the eggs.
Then put the mixture obtained in a piping bag. Arrange on parchment paper or a
flexiplaque, spacing well. Tap the plate to flatten the cookies and expel the air. Set
aside in the open air for about 1 hour (the cookies should no longer stick to your
finger). When the cookies are ready, bake for about 15 minutes at 160°.
Meanwhile, prepare the confit: cook the raspberries with the sugar over low heat.
Soften the gelatine in cold water for 10 minutes. When the coulis is ready, add the
gelatine leaves one by one, mixing well. Let the mixture set in a cool place.
5.put the confit in a piping bag, and garnish the cookies in the center.

The American cookies !
cookies: 25

Preparation time: 15 min

Ingredients

226g butter
150g white sugar
160g brown sugar
2 eggs
1 teaspoon vanilla extract
295g of flour
1 teaspoon of bicarbonate
1 pinch of salt
200g of chocolate or pastry chocolate cut into pieces

Preparation

Utensils :
- mixer (hand mixer...)
- baking sheet
- parchment paper
- spatula
Preparation:
- prepare the baking sheet and preheat the oven to 190°C.
- In a large bowl, work the butter into a fluffy consistency (using a mixer)
- add the white sugar, mix (with the mixer)

- add the brown sugar, mix (with the mixer)
- add eggs one by one, mixing well with each egg (using the mixer)
- add the vanilla
- in a separate container, mix the flour, baking soda and salt
- add this mixture to the liquid mixture and mix well (using the mixer)
- add the chocolate chips and mix with a spatula.
- put in the fridge for 30 minutes
COOKING:
-put 2 teaspoons of dough on the parchment paper, spacing them well.
- Bake for 5 to 10 minutes: the cookies should be colored around the edges.
Enjoy them warm or cold (they are better cold!)

Cookies Levain Bakery way
size of cookies: 8

Preparation time: 15 min

Ingredients

230g of soft butter at room temperature
130g of vergeoise
100g powdered sugar
2 large eggs
350g wheat flour
30g cornstarch
1 teaspoon of bicarbonate
1 pinch of salt
125g of cracked nuts
250g milk chocolate chips

Preparation

Start by creaming the butter and add the two kinds of sugar. Mix well.
Then add the two eggs and mix until the mixture is homogeneous.
In a separate bowl, mix all the dry ingredients (flour, corn flower, baking powder, baking soda and salt).
Add to the previous mixture and finish by adding the chopped nuts and milk chocolate chips.
Divide the dough into 8 equal portions and shape into high balls on the baking sheet.
These cookies are huge and that's the way it should be! Let the dough balls rest in the freezer for about 15-30 minutes to harden the dough and during this time, preheat the oven to 210°C.
Bake for 9 to 12 minutes at 210°C. They are particularly delicious while still warm with a large glass of milk.

Cranberry Muffins
muffins: 12

Preparation time: 15 min

Ingredients

230g cranberries (fresh or frozen), coarsely chopped
140g sugar
25g butter or margarine
1 egg
125ml milk
230g flour
1 pinch of salt
1 level teaspoon of yeast

Preparation

Preheat the oven to Th 6 (180°C).
1 - Cream the butter with the sugar. Add the egg and mix.
2 - In another bowl, mix flour, yeast, salt and milk.
3 - Add the butter-sugar mixture to the previous mixture. Mix well.
4 - Add the cranberries.
5 - Fill muffin tins 3/4 full and bake for 25-30 minutes, until golden brown.

Lemon muffins
muffins: 12

Preparation time: 10 min

Ingredients

230g flour
110g sugar
1 tablespoon baking powder
1 teaspoon of salt
1 egg
8cl melted butter
Lemon
15cl of milk
lemon zest

Preparation

Preheat the oven to 200°C (thermostat 6-7).
Mix the flour, sugar, yeast and salt and make a well in the center.
Beat the egg in another bowl. Add the melted butter, milk, zest and juice.
Pour this mixture into the well and stir.
Pour into muffin tins and bake for 20 minutes.

Almond and cherry muffins
Muffins: 20

Preparation time: 35 min

Ingredients

230g flour
125g almond powder
75g of sugar
1 packet of baking powder
1 egg
25cl of milk
1/2 teaspoon almond extract
50g of almonds
200g of cherries
1 pinch of salt

Preparation

Mix the flour, sugar, yeast and pinch of salt. In a separate bowl, beat the egg
lightly and then gradually add the milk and almond extract.
Preheat the oven to 170°C (gas mark 5/6).
Mix the two preparations. Toast the slivered almonds for 5 to 7 minutes.
Stir the almonds and chopped cherries into the mixture, pour into the muffin
cups and bake at 200°C (gas mark 6/7) for 20 to 25 minutes.

Chocolate chip and nutella muffins
Muffins: 12

Preparation time: 10 min

Ingredients

230g of flour
140g sugar
50g of butter
1 egg
1 sachet of yeast
125ml of milk
1 pinch of salt
120g of chocolate
125g of chocolate (for the dough)
12 spoonfuls of nutella coffee

Preparation

Recipe to be prepared in two parts. The liquid part and the solid part.
Preheat the oven to 180°C (thermostat 6)
LIQUID PART
Melt the butter and the chocolate in a bain-marie.
Once melted, add the milk and the egg.
SOLID PART

In another container, mix flour, salt, sugar, yeast and chocolate chips.
Add the liquid part to the solid part.
CAUTION: For beautiful muffins, it is important that the batter
is not smooth. You must mix very roughly.
Don't be afraid to leave lots of lumps.
Fill 1/3 of your molds with your preparation.
Add a teaspoon of nutella to the center and cover the remaining 2/3 with the batter.
Bake for 15 to 20 minutes depending on your oven.
It is important not to open the oven before the end of the cooking
time or your muffins will fall apart.
Let cool for 10 to 15 minutes before unmolding.
For more ease, I recommend a silicone mold.
All that's left to do is enjoy!

Orange blossom cannelés

cannelés: 20

Preparation time: 20 min

Ingredients

230g of flour
450g of sugar
4 eggs
1/2l of boiling milk
1/4 cold milk
1 tablespoon orange blossom
1 tablespoon vanilla liquid
2 tablespoons rum

Preparation

Mix together the flour with the sugar; then, add the 4 eggs.
Boil 1/2 liter of milk... and add it gradually to the mixture.
Immediately after (important!), pour 1/4 liter of cold milk. Mix well.
Then add the orange blossom, the liquid vanilla and the rum.
Butter the molds (even silicone ones), and pour the preparation into them.
Bake for 10 minutes at 240°C, and then 35 to 40 minutes at
180°C... Do not open the oven during baking!

Blueberry Muffins

small muffins: 20

Preparation time: 15 min

Ingredients

230g of frozen blueberries
140g sugar
25g of butter

1 egg
125ml of milk
230g of flour
1 pinch of salt
1 level teaspoon of baking powder

Preparation

Preheat the oven to 180°C (thermostat 6).
Mix the butter with the egg and the milk.
In another container, mix sugar, flour, salt and baking powder.
Mix the two mixtures together, but do not stir too much even if the
dough is not very smooth. You want to leave some lumps!
Add the still frozen blueberries and mix well.
Fill the muffin tins 3/4 full and bake for 25 to 30 minutes until golden brown.

Chocorangettes (chocolate-glazed orange madeleines)
madeleines: 20

Preparation time: 15 min

Ingredients

230g powdered sugar
150g butter
3 juicy oranges
3 eggs
125g of flour
2 teaspoons baking powder
1 pinch of salt
100g of dark chocolate

Preparation

In a tray with 20 impressions (madeleine mold, if possible flexible)
Mix in this order: sugar, butter, orange zest, orange juice (use 10 cl, then reserve
the rest), the 3 eggs one by one, flour, baking powder and salt.
Fill the moulds 3/4 of the way and cook for 10 to 15 minutes in a preheated oven at 175°C.
Turn out and let cool. Sprinkle the cold madeleines with the remaining orange juice.
Melt a little chocolate in a bain-marie and, using a brush, brush them on their fluted part.

Almond and orange cakes
Serves: 6

Preparation time: 10 min

Ingredients

240g almond powder

120g of powdered sugar
6 eggs
50g of flour
Orange
processed orange peel
1/2 sachet of baking powder
1 pinch of salt
20g of butter

Preparation

Preheat the oven to 180°C (thermostat 6).
Butter the pan carefully. Mix the flour and the yeast.
Break the eggs and separate the whites from the yolks.
Whisk the yolks with the sugar until the mixture turns slightly white.
Add a pinch of salt to the whites and beat them until stiff with the whisk of your electric mixer.
Add the powdered almonds to the first mixture, then pour in the orange juice and zest and gradually add the egg whites, coating them with the batter in a wide gesture to avoid breaking them.
Fill the mold with this paste and put in the oven for 50 minutes.
Let cool and cut into small pieces.

New Zealand coconut and macadamia nut cookies
pieces: 25

Preparation time: 20 min

Ingredients

240g butter
140g sugar
160g brown sugar
1 egg
170g flour
100g oatmeal
1 teaspoon of baking powder
1 pinch of salt
60g of grated coconut
120g macadamia nuts

Preparation

Coarsely chop the macadamia nuts and set aside.
Preheat the oven to 180°, thermostat 6.
In a bowl, combine the sugar, brown sugar and egg. Beat the mixture well.
In a separate bowl, soften the butter with a spatula to make it creamy.
Add to base mixture and continue to beat well.
In another bowl, combine flour, oats, baking powder and salt.
Add the first mixture to this one, still beating to obtain a smooth cream.

Add the grated coconut and the chopped macadamia nuts.
On a baking sheet lined with parchment paper, place small balls the size of a
mirabelle plum. Remember to space the balls of dough far enough apart!
Bake for about 15 minutes until the edges are golden. The
center of the cookies should still look soft.
Let cool in the oven for 30 minutes before removing from the oven.

Easter Carrot Cupcake
cupcakes: 12

Preparation time: 30 min

Ingredients

240g of carrots to obtain 200g of grated carrots
130g of brown sugar
3 eggs
200g of flour
100g of butter
1/2 sachet of yeast
1 teaspoon of bicarbonate
1 pinch of salt

Preparation

To start... we are happy!!! It is so important to cook with a smile... it is the essential ingredient!
Let's make the cakes... too easy!
Preheat the oven to 160°C.
Peel and grate your carrots.
In a large bowl, mix the eggs with the sugar. Your mixture will turn white.
Add the flour, baking powder, baking soda and salt.
Then add your grated carrots and the melted butter.
Guess what?! your dough is ready!
Fill your caissettes to 2/3 and put in the oven for 20 minutes.
You can also make a cake by cooking it for 45 minutes.
The cakes cooked, we decorate them!
Let's start by making the frosting!
Whip the butter with the Philadelphia for 2 minutes. Add the powdered
sugar and mix for 3 minutes, add the liquid vanilla.
Using a piping bag or a spoon, decorate the cupcakes with this icing.
Add small Easter eggs or chocolate sprinkles.
A carrot' cupcake... it makes for a great mood!!!

Lemon - kiwi shortbread
people: 40

Preparation time: 1h30

Ingredients

240g of flour
100g of butter
100g powdered sugar
100g of almond powder
1 lemon (zest)
1 small pinch of saffron powder

Preparation

Lemon saffron sand:
Make a shortcrust pastry by mixing the flour, butter, powdered sugar, almond
powder, lemon zest and saffron powder.
Roll out between 2 sheets of guitar paper, block in the cold.
Cut into 10cm diameter discs with a cookie cutter; bake in silicone
molds at 170°C (Th 5-6) for 15 min.
Crisp feuillantine :
Melt the milk couverture, add the praline and crumbled gavottes, hazelnut paste, and
ointment butter. Roll out between 2 sheets of guitar paper and keep cold.
Cut out disks of the same diameter as the shortcrust pastry base.
Chiboust Kiwi cream :
Make a pastry cream with: the cream, the kiwi pulp, the sugar, the cream powder, the egg yolks.
Remove from the heat and add the kirsch and the gelatine leaves, softened
in cold water and pressed.
Make an Italian meringue:
Cook the sugar at 117°C, pour it on the whites.
Stir the meringue into the still warm pastry cream, then let cool. Train in silicone
molds, embed Morello cherries; block in cold.
Ganache :
Bring cream and invert sugar to a boil; pour over chocolate,
then blend. Blend in butter and set aside.
Assembly :
Place a disc of crispy feuillantine on a shortbread disc. Turn out a puck of chiboust
kiwi cream, caramelize it with an iron (or a blowtorch).
With the ganache, dress around the pocket of small points, put on top
a slice of candied kiwi; coat and decorate as desired.

Chocolate orange cupcakes
Serves 10

Preparation time: 2 min

Ingredients

240g of flour
200g of chocolate powder (amount according to taste)
1 packet of baking powder
75g melted butter

1 glass of milk
120g sugar
drop of orange flavouring

Preparation

Preheat the oven to 210°C.
Mix all the ingredients in the above order.
Pour the mixture into small silicone molds if possible.
Bake for 12 to 15 minutes at 210°C.
It's ready!

Chocolate Coconut Ball Muffins
muffins: 12

Preparation time: 15 min

Ingredients

240g flour
3 teaspoons baking powder
1/2 teaspoon baking soda
4 tablespoons of sweetened cocoa
1 egg
100g of sugar
1 sachet of vanilla sugar
10cl oil or 80g butter
25cl of milk
12 Raffaelo (coconut balls)

Preparation

Preheat the oven to 180°C (thermostat 6). Butter the muffin tin
or place the paper liners in the muffin tin.
In a bowl put the flour, baking powder, bicarbonate and cocoa powder
and stir until you get a uniform mixture.
In another bowl put the egg, powdered sugar, vanilla sugar, oil/butter and milk. Mix well.
Then add flour mixture and mix until dry ingredients are moistened.
Put a tablespoon of batter in each hole of the muffin tin. Place the coconut
ball in the center. Add remaining batter until ball is covered.
Bake for about 20 minutes at 180°C.

Chocolate-banana cookies
cookies: 30

Preparation time: 30 min

Ingredients

240g of flour

60g of oat flakes
110g of sugar
1 pinch of salt
1 sachet of vanilla sugar
1/2 sachet of yeast
100g melted margarine
2 tablespoons of oil (olive)
1 tablespoon of honey
1 egg

Preparation

Preheat the oven to 200°C (thermostat 6-7)
In a bowl, mix all the ingredients one by one: flour, oatmeal, sugar, salt, vanilla sugar, yeast.
Melt the margarine and add it to the other ingredients, then add oil, honey and egg.
Cut banana and chocolate into small cubes and mix again (not too long so as not to make mush).
Shape the cookies with a tablespoon, or - even better - by hand and
place them on parchment paper on the drip pan.
Bake for 15 minutes.
Take them out immediately and let them cool for 5/10 min on a (cold) rack.

Charlotte with pink Reims cookies and raspberries
Serves 8

Preparation time: 20 min

Ingredients

24 spoon cookies or pink cookies from Reims
1 raspberry cake (vahiné type)
500g of cottage cheese
1 egg white
1 tablespoon of sugar
4 sheets of gelatin
Fresh or frozen raspberries

Preparation

Line the charlotte mold with cellophane paper, leaving it hanging over the sides.
Line the bottom and sides with the cookies.
Drain the cottage cheese (at least 1/2 hour).
Whisk together the cottage cheese and raspberry topping.
Soften the gelatin in cold water and melt it in the microwave
with 2 cl of water (10 seconds are enough).
Pour the melted gelatin into the cottage cheese and mix well.
Beat the egg white until stiff with a pinch of salt and add the sugar.
Fold the egg white into the cottage cheese mixture.
Add a few raspberries and pour into the mold, fold the film over the preparation

and put in the refrigerator for at least 4 hours.
Turn out and decorate with raspberries.

Chocolate muffins, lactose free
pieces: 10

Preparation time: 20 min

Ingredients

250farina
100g sugar
2 eggs
1 plate of chocolate
10cl almond milk
1sheep's yogurt
1 sachet of gluten-free yeast
1 drop of vanilla flavouring

Preparation

Beat the eggs with the sugar until the mixture turns white.
Gradually add the flour while mixing.
Add milk, yogurt, baking powder and vanilla flavouring and mix until smooth.
Butter a muffin pan or put small paper cups in it.
Fill each muffin tin with half of the batter, place a square of chocolate
on top and cover with a new layer of batter.
Bake for about 15 minutes in a preheated oven at 180°C (gas mark 6).
Meanwhile, melt a few squares of chocolate in a bain-marie to make a coulis
and decorate the muffins.
Check that the muffins are cooked by sticking a knitting needle into them. If it comes
out dry (except for the chocolate inside), remove the pan and let it cool.

Mouchous, red macaroons
Serves 8

Preparation time: 15 min

Ingredients

250g almond powder
400g powdered sugar
6 egg whites

Preparation

Mix 3 egg whites with the sugar and almond powder.
Beat 3 egg whites until stiff and fold into the remaining batter.
Butter and flour the baking sheet and spread small packets of dough on it or, better,

put a spoonful of dough in each cell of a special silicone mold for macaroons.
Bake for 3 minutes in a very hot oven (240°C), then 20 minutes in a medium oven (160°C).

Oreo cookie balls
balls: 20

Preparation time: 10 min

Ingredients

250g Oreo balls
125g Philadelphia
150g milk chocolate
150g white chocolate

Preparation

Mix the Oreos in a blender or put them in a freezer bag and crush them with a rolling pin.
Mix the crushed Oreos with the Philadelphia until smooth.
Place in the refrigerator for 30 minutes.
Form into walnut-sized balls. Put back in the fridge for 15 minutes.
Melt chocolate in a double boiler or in the microwave. Dip balls in white or
brown chocolate. Put back in the fridge for 15 minutes and serve cool.

Chocolate beet cranberries
Serves 8

Preparation time: 20 min

Ingredients

250g of beet
100g of chocolate
3 eggs
100g sugar
100farina
30g of butter
1 teaspoon of vanilla

Preparation

Preheat the oven to 180°C (thermostat 6).
Peel the beets. Cut them into 4 pieces, plunge them into boiling water and cook them
for 20 minutes, until they are tender. Purée them smooth with a blender.
Use 250 g of puree. The rest can be used for decoration (to taste).
Melt the chocolate in a double boiler.
Mix butter, eggs and chocolate.
Add sugar, vanilla, flour and yeast, then the beet puree.
Put the preparation in fluted moulds (cooking time: +/- 20 min).

Or in a rectangular dish (cooking time: +/- 30 min).
Check with a knife to make sure it is cooked.

Apple-filled cookies (Turkish)

Serves 6

Preparation time: 45 min

Ingredients

250g of butter
1 jar of plain yogurt
1/2pot of sugar
1 packet of baking powder
1 sachet of vanilla sugar
3 glasses of flour or more

Preparation

Mix the butter, yogurt, sugar and vanilla sugar in a bowl.
Add the flour and baking powder. Mix until the dough is no longer sticky.
In a saucepan, add the peeled and grated apples, sugar and cinnamon. Cook for 5 minutes.
Let cool.
Make rolls with the dough cut into 6 pieces.
Roll out the first piece cut in 4: you get 4 triangles.
Add filling to each piece and roll up like a croissant. Repeat for each piece of dough.
Bake at 180°, thermostat 6, for 15 min.
Bon appétit!

Madeleines of Laetitia

madeleines: 54

Preparation time: 15 min

Ingredients

250g of butter
6 eggs
280g caster sugar
310g of flour
Orange blossom

Preparation

1 - Melt the butter in a bowl for 2 minutes in the microwave. Break the eggs into a bowl.
2 - Add the sugar to the eggs and whisk to whiten the mixture.
3 - Mix in the flour, melted butter and orange blossom.
Let this preparation rest in the fridge for 1 hour.
4 - Butter the baking sheets, otherwise prefer silicone baking sheets for 9 madeleines.
Pour in the dough with a small spoon, filling the spaces 3/4 of the way. Bake in

THE FRENCH COOKIE BAKEBOOK

the oven at 190°C for 12 minutes, preferably in a revolving oven.
5 - Turn out the madeleines when they are cooked and let them cool on a rack.

White chocolate, cranberry and pumpkin seed cookies
cookies: 30

Preparation time: 20 min

Ingredients

250g of semi-salted butter
120g brown sugar
1 sachet of vanilla sugar
2 eggs
300g of flour
1 packet of baking powder
230g white chocolate
150g of cranberries
125g pumpkin seeds
1 rum (I use homemade rum)

Preparation

Cut the white chocolate squares in 4.
Beat the butter, brown sugar and vanilla sugar for 30 seconds (until the mixture turns white).
Add the eggs one after the other while continuing to beat.
Add flour and baking powder and mix well.
Add white chocolate and mix with a wooden spoon. Add the cranberries
and pumpkin seeds and mix. Add the rum and mix.
Put 30 minutes in the refrigerator.
Preheat oven to 180°C (gas mark 6).
On a baking sheet, spread baking paper. Using an ice cream scoop, scoop out balls
of dough and place them on the baking sheet, leaving enough space between
each ball so that the cookies don't stick when they spread out.
Bake for 12 to 14 minutes, until golden brown around the edges.

Nutella® sandwich cookies
cookies: 25

Preparation time: 28 min

Ingredients

250g butter
150g powdered sugar
500g of flour
1 egg
1 vanilla bean

200g of Nutella

Preparation

Cut the vanilla bean in half lengthwise and scrape out the seeds. In a bowl, mix the powdered sugar, egg, butter, vanilla seeds and salt until you have a smooth dough.
Add the sifted flour and stir briefly to form a ball and wrap in cling film.
Let the dough rest for one hour in the refrigerator.
Take the dough out of the fridge and cut it in half with a knife, placing each piece of dough between two sheets of baking paper to obtain a thickness of 3 mm.
Let the two pieces of dough rest in the refrigerator for at least 10 minutes (ideally one hour).
Remove both doughs from the fridge.Using the first dough, cut out cookies using a 6cm round cookie cutter.Place them on a baking sheet covered with baking paper.Repeat the process with the second dough using the same cookie cutter. Cut out shapes from the dough using stencils.
Bake the cookies halfway up at 180°C (gas mark 6) for about 8 to 10 minutes.
Take the cookies out of the oven and let them rest.
Using a piping bag, pipe 8g of Nutella® onto each full cookie, then top with the stencilled cookies, pressing down lightly so that the Nutella® comes out lightly in the hollow of the cookie.

Moroccan Almond Cookies
pieces: 30

Preparation time: 10 min

Ingredients

250g butter
200g of raisins
100g of sugar
1 teaspoon of baking powder
3 eggs
3 drops of vanilla
300g of flour
250g almonds broken into small pieces (with skin)

Preparation

In a bowl, mix the butter with the sugar. Then add the raisins and vanilla. Mix well.
Add 3 egg yolks, the baking powder and finally the flour, while mixing the dough with your hands.
Pour the 3 egg whites into a deep dish and the crushed almonds into another dish.
Make balls the size of walnuts and dip in the egg whites, then in the almonds.
Bake in a preheated oven at 160°C for about 30 minutes.

Daisies (small cookies)
Serves 8

Preparation time: 20 min

Ingredients

250g of butter
120g of powdered sugar
4 hard egg yolks
200g cornstarch
200g flour (type 00)
1 pinch of salt
1 finely grated lemon peel

Preparation

Preheat the oven to 200°C (thermostat 6-7).
In a large bowl, beat butter and sugar vigorously.
Add the zest and salt.
Then add the yolks and sift through a fine sieve.
As soon as the mixture is homogeneous, add maizena and flour.
Put the dough in the refrigerator for two hours.
Roll out the dough with a roller (1 cm) and with the help of a small
form, cut out daisies of about 3 cm in diameter.
With your finger, make a small hollow in the center of the flowers.
Place them well spaced on parchment paper.
Bake for about 15 minutes. They should turn golden.
Let cool and sprinkle with powdered sugar.
If there are any left over, they can be stored in a tin.

Cookies with hard caramels and rum
cookies: 35

Preparation time: 10 min

Ingredients

250g of butter
350g powdered sugar
375g of flour
250g deer (hard caramel coated with chocolate)
2 tablespoons of white rum
1 egg
1 sachet of vanilla sugar

Preparation

Mix the brown sugar with the softened butter (be careful, it should not
be melted, just soft enough to be worked with a spoon).
Add the whole egg and vanilla sugar. Mix until the mixture is uniform.
Prepare the deer nuggets by cutting them coarsely with a large knife.
Add all the chips and flour at once to the first mixture. Add the rum. Stop mixing as soon as the
two ingredients are integrated. The mixture must remain powdery and not form an amalgam.
Form small balls from the mixture with your hands. Place them on a baking

sheet and flatten them slightly.
Bake at 190-210°C (gas mark 6-7) for about 10 minutes. The cookies should not be too colourful and they should still be soft when they come out of the oven so that they are not too hard when they are cold again (they should still be quite soft, in fact, and you should wait before taking them off the baking sheet...)

Laura Todd Cookies
Serves 4

Preparation time: 20 min

Ingredients

250g of salted butter
150g white powdered sugar
150g of powdered sugar
320g of flour
300g of dark chocolate
2 eggs
2 packets of vanilla sugar

Preparation

Mix the softened butter with the sugars, the flour and the eggs,
until you get a homogeneous mixture.
Place in the refrigerator for 15 minutes.
Form small balls the size of a large walnut and place on a non-stick baking sheet (or a baking sheet covered with butter or parchment paper).
Bake for 7 minutes in a preheated oven at 180°C (gas mark 6), then take them out.
Be careful: they don't look cooked and that's normal: you must now let them rest and finish cooking (thanks to the thermal inertia of the baking sheet) in the open air.
This way, they remain soft and melt under the tooth.

Banana shortbread
Serves 8

Preparation time: 20 min

Ingredients

250g of shortbread cookies
100g of butter
250ml of fresh cream
Banana
1 can of sweetened condensed milk

Preparation

Cook the closed milk can for an hour and a half in boiling water without interruption and let it cool completely.

Crumble the cookies and add the melted butter, put them in a pie
dish and leave in the fridge for 10 minutes.
Cover this cookie with the caramelized milk and then cover with banana slices.
Whip the fresh cream and cover the whole with it.

Homemade speculoos

Serves 6

Preparation time: 20 min

Ingredients

250g brown sugar
350g of flour
250g of butter
1 egg
5g of salt

Preparation

Mix the softened butter with the brown sugar and the egg.
Add the flour with a spatula.
Let stand for 12 hours.
Roll out rectangles of pasta on a baking sheet 2 to 3 mm thick.
Bake at 140°C for 20 minutes.

Spéculoos

Serves 8

Preparation time: 25 min

Ingredients

250g of brown sugar
350g of sifted flour
5g of bicarbonate
1 egg
Salt
250g of butter

Preparation

Rest the dough for 12 hours.
Put 200 g of butter to soften. Mix 300 g of flour, salt and bicarbonate.
Mix the soft butter with brown sugar and egg. Bring together and let rest for 12 hours.
Butter baking sheets with the remaining butter.
Spread 1/3 of the dough (2 to 3 mm thick) and place on the buttered baking sheets.
Repeat 2 times.
Place in a medium oven at 140°C (gas mark 4-5) for 20 minutes.

They should be golden when removed from the oven.
Serve cold.

Two chocolates & Speculoos
Serves 10

Preparation time: 45 min

Ingredients

250g of milk chocolate
250g white chocolate
250g of dark chocolate
200g of pralinoise
80cl of liquid cream
80g of soft butter
30 peculiar cookies
70g icing sugar
125g flour
125g powdered sugar
4 eggs
1/2 sachet of yeast
1 teaspoon of cinnamon powder

Preparation

Preparation of the sponge cake:
Preheat your oven to 180°C (thermostat 6).
Separate the whites from the yolks, beat the whites until they are stiff and then add the sugar. The whites must be very firm. Reduce the speed of the mixer and add the yolks. Add the flour and baking powder and the teaspoon of cinnamon powder.
Place the dough on a baking sheet lined with buttered baking
paper. The dough should be about 5 mm thick.
Bake for about 10-12 minutes. Remove from oven and let cool while you prepare the mousses.
Preparation of the mousses :
Whip the liquid cream (40cl) until stiff. When you remove the whip,
the cream should form a beak. Keep in a cool place.
Melt the white chocolate in a bain-marie.
Remove the whipped cream from the refrigerator and gently fold the
white chocolate into the cream. Reserve in the freezer.
Repeat this operation with the milk chocolate: whip the liquid cream (40 cl) into a firm whipped cream and set it aside in the fridge. Melt the milk chocolate in a bain-marie, take out the whipped cream and gently fold the milk chocolate into the cream. Reserve in the freezer.
Preparation of the pralinoise:
Melt the pralinoise with the 80 g of soft butter. When it is melted, add to the pralinoise about 10 speculoos previously crumbled. Mix together.
Assembling the cake:

Using a removable cake tin or a pastry ring, place the tin on the sponge cake
and cut out the outside. The sponge cake will be the base of the cake.
Spread the praline on the sponge cake (as thick as you like) and place the mold in
the refrigerator for 10-15 minutes so that the praline hardens a little.
Then, take the cake out of the refrigerator and either use a piping bag or simply a
spoon to spread a good layer of white chocolate mousse and then milk chocolate
mousse almost to the top of the mold (leave about 1 cm).
Set aside in a cool place.
Prepare the mirror glaze:
Melt the dark chocolate in a double boiler. When the chocolate is melted, add the icing
sugar and 5 tablespoons of milk. Mix and set aside for 10-15 minutes in a cool place.
Pour the ganache with a ladle over the cake to cover it completely.
Chill for at least 2 hours before decorating.
To decorate, cut speculoos in half and apply them around the cake.
But you can also let your imagination run wild!

Gourmet muffins from a Vivil: chocolate, walnut and hazelnut
cupcakes: 24

Preparation time: 15 min

Ingredients

250g of chocolate fondant
175g butter
125g sugar
75g of fermenting flour
5 eggs
150g walnut kernel
100g hazelnut powder
1 tablespoon vanilla extract
1 teaspoon of cinnamon powder

Preparation

Preheat the oven to 180°C (gas mark 6).
On one side, melt the chocolate with the butter in the microwave.
Once everything is melted and not too hot, add the eggs and stir well for a few minutes
(those who want can put only the yolks and add the whites at the end of the recipe).
In another dish, mix the sugar, the flour, the hazelnut powder (to be made by
yourself in a mixer with whole hazelnuts) and the walnut kernels that you
crush in your hand beforehand so that it doesn't make too big pieces.
Once the two preparations are done, mix them and finally add the vanilla extract
and the cinnamon.
Place the mixture in muffin tins or in small papers pleated for this purpose
(do not fill to the top, but to 3/4).
Bake for about 15 minutes.

Madeleines with pumpkin
pieces: 30

Preparation time: 15 min

Ingredients

250g of squash (pumpkin or pumpkin)
2 eggs
110g of sugar
250g of flour
125g melted butter
10g baking powder

Preparation

Preheat the oven to 190°C (thermostat 6).
Cut the flesh of the squash in small pieces and cook it in simmering water for 5 minutes.
Drain well and fry in butter for 2 or 3 minutes. Set aside.
Blanch the eggs and sugar together,
add flour and yeast sifted together
then the melted butter (hazelnut is even better) and finally the squash.
Fill the buttered madeleine molds (or silicone molds) with 3/4 of the mixture
and bake for 10 to 12 minutes at 190°C.

Shortbread with fresh cream
shortbread: 25

Preparation time: 10 min

Ingredients

250g of flour
1/2 packet of almond powder (about 70g)
2 egg yolks
1 pint of semi-thick cream (18% fat)
25g white sugar (cane sugar, if possible)
1/2 package of baking powder

Preparation

Preheat the oven to 160°C (th 5-6).
Mix the flour, yeast, sugar, yolks, almond powder and cream to obtain a soft
dough, not sticky to the fingers (add more flour if necessary).
Put in ball. Let rest for 1 hour in the fridge.
Roll out to 5 mm thickness (not more, because they will puff up!), and cut
them out with cookie cutters or small lids (3 or 4 cm diameter).
Bake for about 15 min, watching the color: they can turn golden, but not more,

THE FRENCH COOKIE BAKEBOOK

because even if they don't look cooked, they cool down as they harden!

Real American Cookies

Serves: 4

Preparation time: 5 min

Ingredients

250g flour
1/2 sachet of yeast
125g of white sugar
125g brown sugar
125g melted butter
1 egg
1 packet of vanilla sugar
1 pinch of salt
Chocolate at will

Preparation

In a bowl, mix the flour, yeast, sugars, salt and vanilla sugar.
In a bowl beat the egg and add the melted butter.
Put the butter and egg mixture into the flour and sugar mixture all at once.
Add the chocolate chips (white, dark or milk). Mix with a wooden spoon.
Place in the refrigerator for 1 hour (not necessary).
Preheat oven to 240°C (gas mark 8).
Shape cookies about 5 cm in diameter and 1/2 cm thick.
Place them on a baking sheet covered with parchment paper, spacing them out.
Bake for 10 minutes per batch.
Allow to cool slightly before removing and placing on a rack.
The cookies should be soft in the center and crisp on the edges.

Valentinian shortbread

Serves 6

Preparation time: 30 min

Ingredients

250g of flour
1/2 sachet of baking powder
110g brown sugar (or powdered sugar)
2 eggs
65g melted butter
orange zest
1 tablespoon orange blossom
1 tablespoon of rum

Preparation

In a bowl, pour flour, brown sugar, yeast and mix with a scraper. Make a well.
Add the melted butter, orange zest, eggs, orange blossom and rum.
Mix the whole with the hand until obtaining a paste which does not
stick to the fingers. Add a little flour if it is too wet.
Preheat oven to 170°C.
Roll out the dough (it should be 3 to 5 mm thick) on a sheet of parchment
paper the size of the baking sheet.
Cut out rhombuses with a fluted roulette wheel (or a knife, if you don't have one).
Bake in the oven for 35 minutes.
Cool on a rack.
This cookie can be eaten stale.

Christmas shortbread with Thermomix

Serves 6

Preparation time: 15 min

Ingredients

250g of flour
100g of butter
100g brown sugar
100g almond powder
1 egg yolk
1 egg yolk
1 teaspoon of yeast
Cinnamon
Nutmeg

Preparation

Preheat the oven to 180°C (thermostat 6).
Put the sugar and the butter cut in pieces in the Thermomix. Add the
whisk and heat for 3 minutes at 35°C on speed 2.
Add the flour, baking powder, almond powder, spices and egg. Mix again for 2 minutes on speed 4.
Scrape down the sides of the bowl and collect the dough. Work
the dough by hand until it is homogeneous.
Roll out the dough on a floured work surface with a rolling pin.
Then cut out the shortbread with a cookie cutter.
Arrange the shortbread on a baking sheet covered with parchment paper.
Brush the top of the cookies with the egg yolk. Dilute with a spoonful of milk, if necessary.
Place in the oven for 10 minutes, keeping an eye on the cooking time.
Let the shortbread cool before eating.

Fig shortbread

THE FRENCH COOKIE BAKEBOOK

Serves 6

Preparation time: 30 min

Ingredients

250g of flour
100g of butter
1 egg
2 tablespoons of liquid cream
100g of powdered sugar

Preparation

Preparation of the fig paste.
Remove the tails from the dried figs.
In a saucepan, mix the figs with the vanilla sugar and 2 tablespoons of water.
Cook over low heat for 25 to 30 minutes.
Mix the preparation.
Return the mixture to the saucepan and heat again to dry out the paste.
Set aside in a cool place.
Preparation of the filled cookies.
Beat the egg and sugar until the mixture turns white.
Add sugar and cream and mix well.
Mix in the butter and flour and knead the dough by hand.
Form a ball, wrap in cling film and chill for 1 hour.
Preheat oven to 150°C (gas mark 5).
Roll out the dough with a rolling pin.
In the center of the dough, spread the fig paste.
Fold over the edges of the dough, sticking well edge to edge.
Cut the resulting sausage into several pieces to form the cookies.
Place the cookies on a baking sheet covered with baking paper, with the closed side of the cookies on the sheet, and bake for 30 minutes.

Macaroon-style tartlets
Serves 15

Preparation time: 25 min

Ingredients

250g flour
100g of butter
1 pinch of salt
Cold water
3 tablespoons raspberry jelly
2 egg whites
175g powdered sugar
100g ground or powdered almonds

Preparation

Mix flour and salt.
Incorporate the butter divided into pieces by rubbing between the fingertips
and wet with a little water to obtain a soft but firm dough.
Let rest in the refrigerator for at least 1 hour. Roll out the dough with a rolling
pin to 2-3 mm and place in 15 small buttered tartlet pans.
Spread the raspberry jelly on the bottom.
Preheat oven to 180°C (gas mark 6).
Prepare the filling by beating the egg whites until stiff. Add the sugar and almond
powder without stopping beating. Fill the tarts with the mixture.
Bake for 20 to 25 minutes.
Turn out, place on a hot baking sheet and return to the oven for 5 minutes. Let cool or enjoy warm.

Christmas cookies
Serves 6

Preparation time: 15 min

Ingredients

250g of flour
100g of butter
125g of sugar
50g almond powder
1 egg
1 teaspoon of yeast

Preparation

Mix the flour, yeast, sugar and almond powder in a large bowl.
Add the butter and the eggs; then work first with a fork and then with your hands.
Season to taste with 4 spices, cinnamon/orange, lemon...
I cut the ball in 3, and I make 3 different seasonings!
Preheat the oven to 200°C (thermostat 6-7).
Roll out the dough with a rolling pin and cut out shapes with a cookie cutter
(fir trees, moons, stars......).
Place them on a baking sheet lined with parchment paper.
Spread a little egg yolk with cinnamon on the cookies, so that they are golden brown.
Place in the oven for 7 to 10 minutes (to be watched).

White chocolate and red fruit cookies
cookies: 15

Preparation time: 15 min

Ingredients

250g flour
100g brown sugar
1 pinch of salt
1 sachet of vanilla sugar
half of yeast
1 egg
125g of butter
1 teaspoon of honey
White chocolate (to be cut in small pieces, quantity according to your wishes)
Soft red fruits (quantity according to your taste)

Preparation

In a large bowl, mix the flour, brown sugar, vanilla sugar, salt and yeast.
Melt the butter and add the egg and honey.
Add to the first bowl.
Add the white chocolate chips and the red fruits. Mix with a large wooden spoon.
Preheat the oven to 220°C (thermostat 7-8)
Make the cookies. Place them on a baking sheet initially covered with parchment paper. It is important to leave some space between your cookies because they will grow during the baking process.
Put in the oven
For really soft cookies, the baking time will be 9 minutes.
You can leave them a little longer if you like them crispier (max 11min)
Bon appétit!

Chocolate chip & peanut butter cookies
Serves 4

Preparation time: 20 min

Ingredients

250g of flour
120g of caster sugar
1/2 sachet of baking powder
1 sachet of vanilla sugar (or better vanilla extract)
1 pinch of salt
100g melted butter
2 eggs
200g of peanut butter
Chocolate to your liking
2 tablespoons of milk

Preparation

Preheat the oven to 190°C (thermostat 6).
In your favorite bowl, mix the flour, caster sugar and vanilla sugar, baking powder and salt.

Add the beaten eggs and the melted butter and mix.
It's time to add the peanut butter and chocolate chips. Yummy!
If necessary, pour in a little milk to loosen the dough, which should be able to be shaped into small balls without sticking to your fingers or crumbling.
On a grid covered with parchment paper, place balls of dough in the size of your choice (your choice!), spacing them out a little.
Bake for 8 minutes for soft cookies.
Hmm it smells good ... !
Once out of the oven, gently peel them off and let them cool on a rack (I always eat one at this stage...).
Bon appetit!

3 Chocolate Cookies with Maple Syrup
Large Cookies: 12

Preparation time: 15 min

Ingredients

250g flour
120g brown sugar
15g of white sugar
1/2 sachet of yeast
1 egg
60g of soft butter
60g of semi-salted butter
2 tablespoons of maple syrup
100g of chocolate
12 squares of chocolate of your choice

Preparation

Preheat your oven to thermostat 7 (210°C).
In a bowl, mix the flour and the 2 sugars. Then add the yeast and mix again.
In a bowl, melt the 2 butters together. In another bowl, mix the egg and the maple syrup. Add the melted butter to the mixture.
Then, mix the 2 preparations energetically with a wooden spoon (avoid the whisk, all the preparation gets stuck in it).
Add the 3 chocolate chips.
Make balls of dough big enough, flatten them and put the chocolate square of your choice. Close the dough and put them on your baking sheet with parchment paper. Space them out well because they flatten out when cooked.
Bake for 10/11 min.
Bon appétit!

Shortbread with peanuts
Serves: 4

Preparation time: 15 min

Ingredients

250g of flour
125g of butter
100g of powdered sugar
1 egg
1/2 teaspoon of bicarbonate
1/2 teaspoon of vanilla or a bag of vanilla sugar
200g of roasted salted peanuts

Preparation

Mix flour, sugar, bicarbonate and vanilla.
Make a well, break the egg and add the butter.
Work until you obtain a homogeneous paste, then add the peanuts.
Form 3 balls, wrap them in plastic film and put them in the freezer for 30 minutes.
Preheat oven to 200°C (gas mark 6-7).
With a knife, cut the sausages into slices about 5 mm thick.
Place them on a baking sheet covered with aluminum foil. Bake for 15 to 20 minutes.
You can also add nuts, raisins, chocolate chips (100g), toasted sesame seeds (100g).

Rolled shortbread with apples, raisins and nuts
Serves 8

Preparation time: 30 min

Ingredients

250g of flour
125g of butter
1 egg
750g of apples (preferably reinette)
100g of powdered sugar
1 bag of walnut kernels
1 bag of raisins
3 spoons of calvados
1 pinch of cinnamon
Salt

Preparation

Put the raisins in the calvados and let them soak for at least 30 minutes.
Mix the flour, the egg, 1 pinch of salt and the softened butter, form a ball and let it rest.
Peel, core and cut the apples into pieces.
Cook them with the sugar and cinnamon.
Add the chopped walnut kernels and the raisins and the calvados they have soaked in.
Roll out the dough with a rolling pin, add the apple-nut-raisin mixture and roll the dough on itself.
Put it on a baking sheet covered with parchment paper and bake

for 30 minutes at 200°C (thermostat 6-7).
Serve warm and sprinkle with powdered sugar.

Breton cider palets
cookies: 20

Preparation time: 30 min

Ingredients

250g of flour
125g of semi-salted butter
75g of brown sugar
50g of white sugar
5cl of cider
2 egg yolks

Preparation

Before you start, you should know that the cider will bring very little in terms of taste.
It will just give a certain crispness to your palet.
In a bowl, mix the flour and sugars.
Add the butter cut into pieces and start mixing until you get a sandy mass.
Add one egg yolk and mix.
Add the cider little by little until you obtain a homogeneous dough (the quantity
of cider varies according to the size of the egg and the quality of the flour).
Roll out the dough until it is 0.5 cm high and cut out circles with a cookie cutter or a small glass.
Place your cookies on the baking sheet.
Brown with the second egg yolk and bake in a preheated oven at 240°C for 20 minutes.
Serve cold.

Garfield's cookies
small cookies: 75

Preparation time: 15 min

Ingredients

250g flour
125g butter
125g of sugar
50g of dark chocolate
1egg
Milk

Preparation

Beat the brown sugar and the egg, the mixture must become foamy.
Add the flour and the dark chocolate chips, and mix, the mixture must be sandy.

Add the soft butter, mix, the mixture must be homogeneous and solid.
Make a ball with the dough.
Spread on baking paper, the dough should be 5 to 7 millimeters thick.
Put the parchment paper on a plate.
Preheat oven to 210°C (gas mark 7).
Using a cookie cutter 3 to 4 centimeters in diameter, cut out the cookie dough.
Brush all the small pieces with milk.
Put in the oven, the cookies must be golden.

Small nut cookies for tea
cookies about: 30

Preparation time: 20 min

Ingredients

250g of flour
125g of butter
100g of brown sugar
1 egg
1/2 teaspoon of bicarbonate
200g of coarsely ground walnuts

Preparation

Mix the flour, the bicarbonate of soda and the sugar in a bowl. Make a well and break the egg into it.
Add the butter. Work until you obtain a smooth and homogeneous paste. Incorporate the nuts.
Roll into two balls. Wrap in cling film. Let rest 30 minutes in the freezer.
Preheat oven to 200°C (gas mark 5).
With a sharp knife, cut the rolls of dough (removed from the film) into 0.5 cm thick slices.
Place the cookies on a baking sheet covered with parchment paper, spacing them
about 2 cm apart. Bake in the oven at mid-height for 15 to 20 minutes.
When they come out of the oven, slide them onto a rack and let them cool completely.

Shortbread galette (giant shortbread!)
Serves 6

Preparation time: 10 min

Ingredients

250g of flour
125g of salted butter
125g of sugar
1 egg + 1 white
1 egg yolk to brown
1 bean!

Preparation

Preheat the oven to 200°C (thermostat 6-7).
Mix the soft butter with the sugar. Add the whole egg and the white, then the flour.
Sand the dough and continue mixing to obtain a ball. Roll out the dough into a large disk.
Brown with egg yolk and bake for about 25 minutes.

Chocolate chip - hazelnut muffins
muffins: 12

Preparation time: 15 min

Ingredients

250g flour
125g dark dessert chocolate crushed into large chips with a hammer
100g hazelnuts, also crushed with a hammer (be careful not to crush them into powder!)
1/2 sachet of baking powder

Preparation

Preheat the oven to 180°C (thermostat 6).
Put all the ingredients for the dry mixture in a bowl and mix well. Set aside.
Put the butter in a saucepan and melt it on a very low heat.
In another bowl, beat the eggs with the sugars until the mixture turns white.
Add the melted and cooled butter.
Pour the wet mixture onto the dry mixture without stirring too
much. Some lumps will remain but this is normal.
Pour this mixture into muffin tins, filling them 2/3 full.
You can add the flaked almonds on the muffins if you wish.
Put in the oven for 20 minutes at 180°C.

Shortbread almonds and calvados
pieces: 30

Preparation time: 10 min

Ingredients

250g of flour
125g almond powder
180g of butter
2 egg yolks
120g of sugar
3 tablespoons of calvados
pinch of salt

Preparation

Preheat the oven to 150°C (thermostat 5).
Pour the flour, almond powder, sugar, salt, egg yolks, calvados and melted butter.

Mix well, first with a wooden spoon and then by hand.
The dough should be a bit sandy!
Roll out the dough and make shapes with cookie cutters or form small croissants.
Bake for 15 minutes.
The shortbread should be barely browned so it stays as melting as you want it to be!

Montecaos
cupcakes: 16

Preparation time: 5 min

Ingredients

250g flour
125g sugar
125g grape seed oil (1g=1ml)

Preparation

Preheat the oven to 180°C.
Mix the flour and the sugar then add the oil and continue mixing.
Make balls with the dough (the size of a scallop).
Bake in the oven at 180°C for 5 minutes (cracks should appear
on the top), then lower the oven to 150°C.
Let cool and sprinkle with cinnamon.

Shortbread with jam
Serves 6

Preparation time: 30 min

Ingredients

250g of flour
125g of sugar
125g of butter
1 egg
1 pinch of salt

Preparation

For the shortcrust pastry: beat the whole egg in a dish. Add the sugar and salt.
Stir with a whisk until you obtain a white mixture with a little foam.
Pour into the sifted flour all at once. Mix with a spatula and then with your hands and
crumble it until it becomes sand. Incorporate the butter and knead by hand.
Make a ball and put it in the refrigerator (preferably at the bottom) for one hour.
To make the shortbread: roll out the dough to a thickness of 3 to 5 mm according to your taste.
Cut out your shortbread with a cookie cutter. For each shortbread, make 2 identical shapes,
one with a hole in the middle. Glue these two shapes together and fill the hole with jam...
Brown the shortbread with egg yolk. Spread them on a plate and put them

in a warm oven for 10 to 15 minutes, watching regularly.

Leopard shortbread

pieces: 24

Preparation time: 30 min

Ingredients

250g of flour
125g of sugar
125g of butter
1 egg
35g cocoa powder
20g almond powder

Preparation

Work the butter and sugar with a wooden spoon until you obtain a smooth and homogeneous mixture. Mix in the flour and egg and finish working the dough by hand until it forms a ball.
Separate the ball of dough into 2 parts and then one of the 2 parts again into 2 parts.
Stir the almond powder into the larger ball of dough.
Stir 1 teaspoon of cocoa into a small ball of dough, and the remaining cocoa into the remaining ball of dough.
Make balls of dough with the smaller ball of dough. Wrap these dough balls in the high cocoa dough.
Roll out the almond powder dough and cut out as many rectangles as there are cocoa puffs.
Wrap each boudin in a rectangle of white dough and then assemble all the boudins to form a single large boudin.
Roll up the resulting boudin to smooth the edges, wrap in cling film and freeze for 30 minutes.
Preheat oven to 180°C (gas mark 6).
Remove the film and cut the roll into thick slices.
Place the slices on a baking sheet covered with baking paper and bake for 15 minutes.
Allow to cool before serving.

Schokobredle (chocolate Christmas cookies)

pieces approx.: 100

Preparation time: 5 min

Ingredients

250g flour
125g sugar
125g melted butter
50g of dark chocolate
1 lemon thread or some zest
1/2 teaspoon baking soda

3 egg yolks for gilding + 1/2 sachet of vanilla sugar

Preparation

Mix flour, sugar, butter, chocolate, lemon and bicarbonate.
Form a ball of dough, roll out half of it to 0.5 cm thickness on a floured work
surface, cut out Christmas shapes and place them on a buttered grid.
Preheat oven to 180°C (gas mark 6).
Gild each piece with egg yolk, then sprinkle with a little vanilla sugar. Decorate as
desired (pieces of candied fruit, lemon or orange peel, flaked almonds...).
Place in the oven for 8 to 12 minutes depending on the type of oven and the desired cooking time.

Chocolate montécaos
montécaos: 20

Preparation time: 5 min

Ingredients

250g of flour
125g of sugar
45g of chocolate powder
125ml of oil (grape seed oil is preferable)

Preparation

Preheat the oven to 180°C (thermostat 6).
Mix the flour, sugar and oil in this direction.
Make balls with the dough.
Bake for 5 minutes. It's ready!

Cookies with chocolate chips and nougatine
cookies about: 20

Preparation time: 15 min

Ingredients

250g of flour
125g powdered cannery sugar
2 packets of vanilla sugar (2 x 7,5g)
1 pinch of salt
1/2 sachet of yeast (6 g)
1 egg
125g of butter
1 tablespoon of milk
2 teaspoons of honey
50g of nougatine chips
100g of chocolate (or more according to your taste)

Preparation

Preheat the oven to 150°C (thermostat 5).
In a bowl, mix the flour, brown cane sugar, vanilla sugar, baking powder and salt.
Melt the butter in a double boiler or in the microwave for 45 seconds (900W), add it to your preparation. Add your beaten egg. Mix well with your whisk until you obtain a smooth paste.
Add a tablespoon of milk and 2 teaspoons of honey. Mix everything together.
Add the nougatine chips and then the chocolate chips.
Mix everything with a wooden spoon so as not to crush them.
Line a grid with baking paper.
Take the equivalent of a tablespoon of your preparation and spread
it over a 7cm diameter to shape your first cookie.
Repeat the process for the other cookies, remembering to space them out.
Place your rack in the oven for 8 to 10 minutes on the second notch
from the bottom. Make the other batches... Enjoy!

American Raisin Muffins

muffins: 12

Preparation time: 20 min

Ingredients

250g flour
125g powdered sugar
1/2 sachet of baking powder
1 pinch of salt
1 egg beaten
25cl of milk
60g melted butter
100g of currants

Preparation

Soak the currants in lukewarm water for about 15 minutes and preheat
the oven to 180°C (gas mark 6).
Meanwhile, mix the flour, yeast, salt and sugar in a bowl.
In a large bowl, beat the egg with the milk and add the melted butter.
Add the contents of the bowl to the bowl.
Mix gently but do not stir too long.
Drain the grapes on a paper towel, lightly flour them (so they don't fall to
the bottom of the molds) and then add them to the batter.
Fill the moulds 3/4 full and bake for 25 minutes.

Back to school shortbread

Serves 6

Preparation time: 25 min

Ingredients

250g of flour
125g of caster sugar
1 egg
100g of butter
1 lemon peel
1 pinch of salt
Sugar paste of different colors (at least 3, pink / green / yellow / blue)
Powdered sugar

Preparation

In a bowl, mix the egg with the powdered sugar and a pinch of salt.
In a bowl, pour the egg, make a well in the center, pour in the contents
of the bowl and the lemon zest.
Knead until you have a homogeneous dough.
Roll out the shortbread dough to a thickness of 3 mm and
leave to rest in a cool place for 30 minutes.
Preheat the oven to 180°C (thermostat 6).
When the dough has hardened, cut 2 cm wide strips, and cut the length to obtain
the desired pencil size.
For each strip of dough, cut one end into a point (to form the lead of the pencil).
Place on a baking sheet lined with baking paper and bake for 12 minutes.
Let cool.
Roll out the sugar dough and cut strips of dough the size of shortbread pencils,
but without the tip (so a little shorter!).
Cut the top of one end of the strips with a notched cookie cutter
to match the pencil pattern you are cutting.
Mix powdered sugar and a little water.
Brush one side of the shortbread pencils with the sugar mixture
and then place a colored sugar paste strip on top.
Finally, cut off the tip of the pencils and place a tip of the right
color sugar paste on top (it's the lead!).

Chocolate Chip and Nutella Cookies
Servings: 12

Preparation time: 15 min

Ingredients

250g flour
130g brown sugar
50g of caster sugar
130g of butter
100g of chocolate

1 egg
12 spoonfuls of coffee of nutella
1 sachet of yeast

Preparation

Preheat the oven to 180° (Thermostat 6)
Melt the butter, add the brown sugar and white sugar with the melted butter and mix.
Add the egg to the preparation, add the yeast to the flour and then gradually add the flour to the rest of the preparation and mix well, add the chocolate chips.
Make a ball in the palm of your hand and flatten it to put a small spoon of nutella in the center then enclose the nutella by making a ball.
Place them on a baking sheet with aluminum foil or parchment paper and bake for 10-15 min.

Lavender shortbread
Serves 8

Preparation time: 15 min

Ingredients

250g of flour
140g butter cut into cubes
100g of caster sugar
1 pinch of salt
1 sachet of vanilla sugar or vanilla flavoring
1 egg yolk
1 level tablespoon of edible lavender

Preparation

On the work surface, place your flour, vanilla sugar, salt and sugar and then incorporate with your hands all the butter until you obtain a grainy paste.
At this point add the egg yolk. When the mixture is homogeneous, add the dried lavender.
Heat the oven to 180°C (thermostat 6). Make a sausage with the dough, and let it rest for 20 minutes in the fridge.
Once ready, cut out circles of a little less than 1 cm and place them on greaseproof paper to cook for 20 min (watch, they are ready when they brown slightly).
Let cool and here are the gourmands!

Apple Cinnamon Muffins
Muffins: 15

Preparation time: 15 min

Ingredients

250g flour
140g of sugar
1 packet of baking powder

125ml of milk
50g melted butter
2 eggs
3 apples (preferably golden)
1 teaspoon cinnamon powder
1 pinch of salt
brown sugar for the finish

Preparation

Preheat the oven to 180° fan oven. (thermostat 6)
Peel and dice the apples, set aside.
In a bowl, mix the dry ingredients: flour, cinnamon, sugar, yeast
and a pinch of salt (separate from the yeast)
In a second bowl, mix the liquid ingredients: milk, melted butter and eggs.
Add the second mixture to the first, stir, then when the mixture is almost smooth
add the apple pieces and mix gently so as not to crush the apples.
Pour into muffin tins up to 3/4 of the way up, then sprinkle a little brown sugar on top
of the muffins to get a slight crunch, bake for 25/30 min at 180° revolving heat.
The muffins must be puffed up and golden at the end of the cooking time, prick a
muffin with a knife to check the cooking, the knife must come out clean.

Christmas cakes with jam
Serves 8

Preparation time: 20 min

Ingredients

250g of flour
150g of butter
100g of sugar
1 egg
Salt
Lemon
Blackberry and redcurrant jam for the garnish

Preparation

Mix all the ingredients.
Form a ball.
Let the dough rest overnight in the refrigerator.
Preheat the oven to 180°C (gas mark 6).
Roll out the dough with your hands to form a sausage of about 3 cm in diameter. Cut
with a knife into 1 cm thick slices. Place the slices on a baking sheet with parchment
paper, then with a finger make a small hole in each slice to put the jam in.
Put a little jam in the hole.
Put in the oven for 15-20 min.

Shortbread from Caen
shortbread: 35

Preparation time: 15 min

Ingredients

250g of flour
150g of butter
75g of sugar
2 hard-boiled eggs (you're not dreaming!)
1 beaten egg yolk
2 tablespoons of milk
1 pinch of vanilla powder

Preparation

Crush the hard-boiled egg yolks with a fork, milk and vanilla powder.
Put the flour on a work surface with the sugar, mix and make a well.
Add the butter in small pieces and the egg yolks and knead with your fingertips.
Once the ingredients are mixed, form a ball and mill the dough 2 or 3
times (milling consists in crushing the dough ball little by little with
the palm of the hand to make the dough homogeneous).
Form a ball and place in the fridge for 2 hours in cling film.
Take the dough out and let it warm up to become soft again.
Preheat your oven to 200°C.
Roll out on a floured surface, cut out with a cookie cutter or with a glass.
Gild with beaten egg yolk and bake for 8 to 10 minutes (when golden).

Muffins with speculoos paste
muffins: 12

Preparation time: 20 min

Ingredients

250g flour
150g brown sugar
80g melted butter
half of yeast
2 eggs
20cl of milk
1 sachet of vanilla sugar
1 pinch of salt
1 nut of speculoos dough per muffin (in supermarkets, in the spread section)

Preparation

In a bowl, mix the flour, sugar, vanilla sugar, salt and yeast.

In a second bowl, whisk the eggs with the milk and melted butter.
Add the mixture from the second bowl to the first bowl. Mix briefly. Your batter
should not be too smooth, if there are lumps it's fine!
Butter your muffin tins (if they are not silicone). Fill your muffin tins 2/3 full as follows:
Fill 1/3 of the molds with muffin batter, then place 1 dab of speculoos batter in the
center of the molds and finally cover the top with 1/3 of the muffin batter.
Bake at 180°C (gas mark 6) for 20 minutes. Keep an eye on the cooking (the top of the muffins
must be well puffed up and golden). Let cool for 5 to 10 minutes before unmolding.

Prune and white chocolate cookies
cookies: 25

Preparation time: 20 min

Ingredients

250g of flour
150g white chocolate, chopped
150g of pitted pruneaumoelleux
125g of butter
170g sugar (brown is better)
1 egg
3 tablespoons of rum
1 packet of baking powder
1 pinch of salt
glass of mustard (and even more if you like it) oatmeal

Preparation

Cut the chocolate into squares, then into small cubes (with a sharp knife, it's easy).
Dice the prunes.
Preheat the oven to 160-170°C (gas mark 5-6).
Mix the butter and sugar until the mixture turns white.
Add the egg, flour, salt, baking powder and rum. Mix well.
Mix in the chocolate and prune cubes, plus any oat flakes.
On a sheet of parchment paper, on a buttered baking sheet or better yet, on a silicone
mat, place small piles of dough (a teaspoon or a tablespoon of dough depending on
the size you want to get for your cookies). The space you should leave between two
cookies is about the size of a cookie. Flatten the top of the cookies slightly.
Bake for about 12 minutes at 170°C.
Cookies can be stored in an airtight box.
A little tip: to prevent them from getting wet, place a cap of aspirin or effervescent
Vitamin C at the bottom of the box.

Vegan shortbread cookies
people: 8

Preparation time: 25 min

Ingredients

250g of flour
150g of margarine
50g of brown sugar
1 good pinch of salt
2 tablespoons of water
1 level teaspoon of liquid vanilla extract

Preparation

Mix together flour, sugar and salt.
Add the margarine, in pieces, and knead the dough until it becomes crumbly.
Add the water and vanilla and mix until you get a homogeneous dough.
Roll into a ball and let the dough rest, covered, for 30 minutes.
Roll out the dough on a floured work surface with a rolling pin or more roughly
with the palms of your hands to a thickness of about 5-7 mm.
Preheat the oven to 160°C (gas mark 5-6), cut out the dough with a cookie cutter and place the
shortbread on a baking sheet covered with baking paper. To decorate the top, use a fork.)
Bake for 15 minutes.
Let cool on a rack.

Banana and chocolate chip muffin
large muffins: 8

Preparation time: 10 min

Ingredients

250g flour
150g sugar
100g butter
15g almond powder
1 half of yeast
2 bananas
100g of chocolate
2 eggs
1 teaspoon vanilla extract or a packet of vanilla sugar

Preparation

Preheat your oven to 180°C (thermostat 6).
Mix the flour, almond powder, chocolate chips and baking powder in a bowl.
Beat 2 whole eggs with the sugar in another bowl.
Heat the butter in the microwave for a few minutes.
Mash the bananas with a fork, then add the vanilla, butter, and bananas
to the egg and sugar mixture while stirring.
You have a semi-liquid paste that you pour into the first bowl.

Mix just until you have a smooth batter.
Butter your muffin tins and pour the batter 3/4 of the way into them.
Bake in a hot oven for 25 minutes.

Muffins with Monbazillac and chocolate chips
muffins: 12

Preparation time: 15 min

Ingredients

250g of flour
150g sugar
125g of butter
100g of chocolate
1 egg
15cl of milk
15cl of Monbazillac (white wine)
1 sachet of baking powder
1 sachet of vanilla sugar
2 pinches of salt

Preparation

Preheat the oven to 180°C (thermostat 6).
In a first bowl, mix the flour, baking powder, chocolate chips and salt.
Melt the butter in the microwave, then in a second bowl, beat the
egg with the sugar, milk, wine and melted butter.
Stir into the first mixture.
Pour the batter into the muffin tins, and let them bake for 15-20 minutes!

White chocolate/chocolate marble muffins
muffins: 8

Preparation time: 15 min

Ingredients

250g flour
150g sugar
125g white chocolate
125g baking chocolate
60g of butter
250ml of milk
1/2 sachet of yeast

Preparation

Mix the flour, yeast and sugar in a bowl.
Divide the butter into two small containers. Add the white chocolate in one

container and the dark chocolate in the other. Melt in the microwave.
Mix the milk with the rest of the first preparation.
Separate it in two to have an identical quantity.
Incorporate in each of the preparations, the butter and the melted chocolate.
Butter and flour the muffin tins. Fill them to three quarters.
Bake between 20 and 25min depending on taste.
For less fatty muffins, do not put butter but let them cook 15/20min.

Candied lemon ginger muffins

muffins: 12

Preparation time: 10 min

Ingredients

250g of flour
170g sugar
100g of butter
20cl of liquid cream
2 eggs
1 lemon (zest + juice)
3 tablespoons candied ginger, coarsely chopped
6g of bicarbonate

Preparation

Preheat the oven to 175°C (thermostat 5-6).
Beat the sugar with the softened butter. Add the lemon zest, then the eggs one by one.
Pour in the cream and lemon juice and beat until the mixture is smooth.
Gradually add the flour and then the bicarbonate.
Finish with the candied ginger cut into small pieces.
Pour into greased muffin tins and bake for 20 minutes.

Shortbread

Serves 6

Preparation time: 15 min

Ingredients

250g of flour
175g of butter
175g of sugar
1 egg
1 sachet of vanilla sugar
1 pinch of salt

Preparation

Beat the egg with the sugar and the pinch of salt until the mixture becomes white.

THE FRENCH COOKIE BAKEBOOK

Add the flour and the butter cut into pieces. Mix until the dough is homogeneous. Put in the oven at thermostat 6 for 10 minutes (or a little more, depending on the oven).

Strawberry and mint muffins
muffins: 12

Preparation time: 10 min

Ingredients

250g flour
180g powdered sugar
1/2 teaspoon of fine salt
1/2 sachet of baking powder
2 eggs
20cl of milk
15cl sunflower oil
125g of strawberries
10 leaves of mint
Butter for the mussels

Preparation

1) Butter the mussels. Sift the flour, salt and yeast into a bowl and make a well.
In another bowl, beat the eggs, powdered sugar, milk and oil.
2) Pour this mixture into the flour and mix quickly.
3) Wash the strawberries, dry them and cut them into small cubes.
Wash and dry the mint leaves, then chop them.
4) Add the mixture to the batter.
5) Divide the mixture between the molds, filling them only 2/3 full.
6) Bake in the oven at half height for 20 to 25 minutes.
7) Remove the muffins from the oven onto a rack and let them cool completely before eating.

Brown sugar cookies
pieces: 30

Preparation time: 30 min

Ingredients

250g flour
190g brown or blond sugar for the desired color
125g of butter
1 teaspoon of 4 spice mix
1 egg
1 teaspoon of yeast

Preparation

Preheat the oven to 180°C (thermostat 6).
Mix everything in order: egg, flour, sugar, melted butter, yeast and spices.
Take a small ball of dough and flatten it in your hand.
Put on baking paper, do not stick them together.
Cook in the oven for 10 to 15 minutes at 180°C (thermostat 6).

The cookies lights

Serves 4

Preparation time: 5 min

Ingredients

250g of flour
19 spoonfuls of sweetener (or equivalent in proportion to 100g of sugar in a measuring cup)
1 sachet of vanilla sugar
1 pinch of salt
1 sachet of yeast
125g of low fat butter (41% fat content)
2 teaspoons of agave syrup (organic section)
50g of chocolate

Preparation

Mix the flour, sweetener, vanilla sugar, and yeast in a bowl.
Melt the low-fat butter, add the beaten egg and the 2 spoonfuls of agave syrup
and then the chocolate chips. Add the whole to the previous mixture.
Mix everything with a wooden spoon.
Preheat your oven to 220°C (gas mark 7-8) with the rack on the bottom.
Shape the cookies to your liking, taking care to space them out for baking.
Bake them for 9 to 11 min depending on how well they are cooked, pay
close attention to how quickly they are cooked at the end.

Crunchy Vanilla Cookies

Serves 4

Preparation time: 10 min

Ingredients

250g of flour
1cl of milk
50g of sugar
50g of butter
1 sachet of vanilla sugar
5cl vanilla liquid
1/2 sachet of baking powder
1 egg yolk

Preparation

Preheat the oven to 180°C (thermostat 6).
In a bowl, mix the flour and the baking powder.
Add the sugar, the vanilla sugar and the softened butter.
Mix to obtain a dough.
Add the milk little by little and mix everything together.
Place the dough in small balls on a baking sheet covered with parchment paper.
Cover the cookies with egg yolk and bake for 20 minutes.

Christmas cookie kit
cookies: 10

Preparation time: 5 min

Ingredients

250g flour
1 teaspoon of bicarbonate
1 teaspoon baking powder
100 chocolate chips
100g oatmeal
100g cane sugar

Preparation

In a bowl, mix the flour, baking powder and bicarbonate. Pour the mixture
into a jam jar. Pack with the back of a tablespoon.
Add in order: oats, press down, white sugar, press down, brown
sugar, press down and chocolate chips, press down.
Close jar and decorate.

Smarties and yogurt muffins
Muffins: 12

Preparation time: 20 min

Ingredients

250g of flour
1 teaspoon baking powder
1/2 teaspoon of bicarbonate
75g of colored chocolate candies (for example Smarties)
1 egg
60g sugar
60ml oil
200g of yoghurt
Powdered sugar (for decoration)

Butter for muffin tray

Preparation

Preheat oven to 180°C. Butter the muffin tray.
Mix flour, baking powder, bicarbonate and 50 g of chocolate candies.
Beat the egg. Add sugar, oil and yogurt and mix thoroughly. Add the flour mixture
and mix well until the dry ingredients are completely absorbed.
Spread the batter evenly in the muffin tray, put in the oven at half
height and bake for about 20 to 25 minutes.
Let the muffins rest for about 5 minutes in the pan.
Then remove from the pan and decorate with the remaining jelly beans before serving.
Now you can enjoy.

Peanut butter and chocolate chip muffins
muffins: 12

Preparation time: 10 min

Ingredients

250g flour
1 egg
80g sugar
25g of butter
250g of peanut butter
25cl of semi-skimmed milk
100g chocolate (to taste)
1/2 sachet of yeast

Preparation

Preheat the oven to 180°C (thermostat 6).
In a bowl, mix together the flour and sugar.
Add the warmed milk, melted butter and egg. Mix together.
Add the peanut butter and beat the mixture until it is smooth.
Add the chocolate chips (don't hesitate to add a sufficient quantity, about 200 g for my part).
Pour the batter into muffin tins and bake for 20 minutes.
Enjoy with a glass of milk.

Chocolate and mint muffins
muffins: 10

Preparation time: 20 min

Ingredients

250g of flour
1 sachet of yeast

THE FRENCH COOKIE BAKEBOOK

1/2 teaspoon of bicarbonate
110sugar (according to your taste)
3 tablespoons of cocoa
1 egg
25cl of milk
2 teaspoons of mint (according to your taste)
50g melted butter

Preparation

Preheat the oven to 200°C (thermostat 6-7).
Heat the milk. When it is hot, add the mint infusions and leave to infuse
for about 10 minutes (depending on how much you like mint).
Meanwhile, in a bowl, mix the flour, sugar, cocoa, baking soda and yeast.
In another bowl, mix the beaten egg and the melted butter. Add the infused milk and mix.
Pour this mixture into the bowl and mix (not too much! the mixture should
not be smooth or the muffins will be elastic, leaving lumps)
Fill the muffin tins (an idea that came to me but that I haven't tested yet is to put a
square of After eight in the heart of the muffin) and bake for 20 to 25 min.

Cookies with essential oils
people: 20

Preparation time: 30 min

Ingredients

250g of flour
1 sachet of yeast
100g of sugar
90g melted butter
50g of powdered almonds
2 eggs
10 drops of edible essential oil

Preparation

Mix the dry ingredients: flour, sugar, yeast, almonds.
Mix in the two eggs.
Melt the butter and add it to the mixture.
Add the essential oil (10 drops for this recipe).
Loosen the dough from the edges of the container to form a ball.
Place in a cool place for about an hour.
Roll out on a well floured surface and cut out shapes with cookie cutters about 0.7cm thick.
The cooking time, in a hot oven 160°C, depends on the size of the cookies and must be supervised.
They will stay shortbread for a long time if kept in an airtight box.
You can then prepare a royal icing, and decorate the cookies with the children.

Marbled chocolate-orange cupcakes
ramekins: 6

Preparation time: 15 min

Ingredients

250g of flour
1 sachet of yeast
10 spoons of melted butter
orange zest
15cl of light cream (1 glass)
1 milk/water
6 squares of chocolate (to melt with a little water or milk)

Preparation

Preheat the oven to 180°C (thermostat 6).
Mix flour, yeast, butter and cream.
Divide the dough in 2:
In one of the 2 parts, pour the juice of the orange and the zest then mix.
In the second part, pour the melted chocolate, add a little milk or water if the dough is too firm.
Butter 6 ramekins and pour in successive layers the orange mixture and the chocolate mixture.
Place in the oven and bake until a knife comes out clean (about 20 minutes).

Nutella cookies
cookies: 20

Preparation time: 20 min

Ingredients

250g of flour
1 sachet of yeast
75g of white sugar
75g cane sugar (brown)
125g melted butter
2 eggs
1 packet of vanilla sugar
Nutella
Chocolate

Preparation

In a bowl, mix flour, yeast, sugar (brown, white and vanilla)
In a bowl, beat the eggs and add the melted butter
Put the eggs and melted butter in the flour mixture.
Then add the Nutella, 3 CS, one by one while mixing

Then add the chocolate chips and mix with a wooden spoon
Preheat oven to 240°.
Make cookies of about 5/6 centimeters in diameter
Place on a baking sheet covered with parchment paper
Bake for about 8 minutes.

Orange shortbread
shortbread: 40

Preparation time: 20 min

Ingredients

250g of flour
1 sachet of baking powder
100g of powdered sugar
1 pinch of salt
100g candied orange peel
1 eggplant
150g of butter

Preparation

In a bowl, mix the flour, yeast, sugar and salt.
Add the orange peels cut in small pieces.
Mix with the egg and the melted butter.
Let stand for about 30 minutes.
Preheat the oven to 180°C (gas mark 6).
Roll out the dough on a floured surface to a thickness of at least half a centimeter.
Using cookie cutters, cut out cookies and bake until lightly browned.

Marbled shortbread
Serves: 6

Preparation time: 20 min

Ingredients

250g of flour
1 sachet of baking powder
150g of fine sugar
1 sachet of vanilla sugar
1 teaspoon of rum
1 egg
120g butter or margarine

Preparation

Sift the flour-yeast mixture on the work surface. Make a fountain and put all the ingredients in it. Knead well to obtain a smooth dough. Divide it into two equal parts.

Mix the chocolate powder, sugar and milk and add this mixture to one of the dough halves.
Roll out the two pieces of dough into two equal rectangles, brush
with egg yolk and place one on top of the other.
Shape the dough into a roll of about 3 cm in diameter AND LEAVE
IN THE COLD FOR AN HOUR until firm.
Cut into 3 mm thick slices and place on a buttered baking sheet.
Bake for about 10 minutes at medium temperature.

Orange Muffins

Serves: 6

Preparation time: 20 min

Ingredients

250g of flour
1 packet of baking powder
150g of white sugar
2 eggs
120g of butter
3 tablespoons of milk
1 tablespoon of orange or flavouring
Orange marmalade
candied orange peel
Powdered sugar

Preparation

Preheat oven to 180°C (gas mark 6).
Mix the flour and yeast separately, then melt the butter in the microwave.
In a bowl, beat the eggs and sugar until the mixture turns white, then add the melted butter.
Then add the flour mixed with the yeast, and stir everything together.
Finally add the orange extract.
Pour the preparation into the muffin tins up to 2/3, then put
in the oven for 20 min at 180°C (Th 6).
At the end of the cooking time, let the muffins cool for 10 minutes, then remove them
from the molds. Open the muffins and fill them with orange marmalade.
For decoration, sprinkle with powdered sugar and decorate with
a piece of candied orange peel and marmalade.

Huge chocolate muffin

Serves 8

Preparation time: 10 min

Ingredients

250g flour

200g sugar
1 egg
1 chocolate bar
120ml of milk
1 yoghurt or 20 cl of light cream
10cl of oil
1 packet of baking powder
2 tablespoons of cocoa powder or nutella

Preparation

Melt the chocolate with the oil and put it aside
Put the flour, sugar and baking powder in a large bowl. And mix well
In another bowl put the milk, the egg and the yoghurt/cream
and mix well then pour in the other mixture
Mix well and add the cocoa/Nutella. Mix well.
Finally, add the melted chocolate and mix.
Bake in the oven at 200°C (thermostat 6-7) for about 50 minutes.
Check the cooking with a knife.

Delicious pear chocolate chip muffins
muffins: 12

Preparation time: 25 min

Ingredients

250g flour
200g sugar
2 eggs
100g of chocolate
2 pears in syrup
100g unsweetened applesauce
1 tablespoon of honey
1 sachet of yeast
1 pinch of salt

Preparation

Preheat the oven to 180°C (gas mark 6).cut the chocolate into chips.cut the pears into cubes.
Beat the eggs with the compote, vanilla, pears and honey. The compote replaces the butter
and allows the realization of muffin (or cake) without fat and thus without complex,
with moreover much taste and softness. This trick of using compote instead of butter
is particularly suitable for fruit desserts and a little less so for chocolate ones.
Mix the flour with the yeast, sugar and chocolate chips. Flouring the chocolate
chips will prevent them from falling to the bottom of the muffin cups.
Make a hole in the center of the dry ingredients (with the flour) and add the egg
mixture. It is important to prepare the dry and wet mixes separately to ensure

that the muffins will be plump after baking.
Mix quickly so that the mixture remains lumpy, this will allow the muffins to puff up well and will prevent the chocolate chips from sinking to the bottom of the moulds.
Using an ice cream scoop, fill the muffin cups 3/4 full. With the ice cream scoop, scoop out balls of muffin batter and place them in the muffin molds. Be careful not to fill the muffin cups more than ¾ full, otherwise you risk overflowing and the muffins will not puff up.
Bake for 20 minutes.

Pistachio muffins with praline heart
muffins about: 20

Preparation time: 15 min

Ingredients

250g of flour
200g powdered sugar
1 sachet of vanilla sugar
100g of butter
100g pistachio paste
3 eggs
20cl of milk
1/2 sachet of baking powder

Preparation

Preheat the oven to 175°C (thermostat 5-6).
First prepare the muffin batter:
Whip the softened butter with the powdered sugar, vanilla sugar and pistachio paste.
Add the whole eggs one by one, whisking briskly between each egg.
Gradually add the sifted flour and milk alternately, so that the dough is not too firm and therefore too difficult to work.
Finally add the baking powder and mix well one last time.
Then prepare the praline heart:
Melt the praline and butter in the microwave (on low power) or in a bain-marie.
Mix well to obtain a smooth and shiny preparation.
Add the sugar, then the whole egg and finally the sifted flour.
Butter and flour a muffin pan (or use a silicone pan).
Pour a large tablespoon of muffin batter into each hole.
With a teaspoon, poke a walnut-sized hole in the middle of each mixture, leaving only a thin film of batter on the bottom of the pan.
Place a heaping teaspoon of praline paste in these holes.
Cover with pistachio paste.
Be careful, the muffins will puff up, so don't fill the molds to the brim but leave a small margin!
Bake in a hot oven for about 20 minutes, keeping an eye on them (the muffins are cooked when a knife blade inserted in them comes out dry).
Let cool or cool completely (depending on taste).

Bon appétit!

Orange Blossom Muffins

Serves: 4

Preparation time: 15 min

Ingredients

250g of flour
250g of butter
250g of sugar
4 eggs
1 pinch of salt
4 tablespoons orange blossom water

Preparation

Melt the butter (about 30 seconds in the microwave).
Beat the eggs until they foam, then add the flour, sugar, salt and orange
blossom water (I do it in a food processor and it works very well).
Finally add the melted butter and mix well.
Let the dough rest for about 1 hour in the fridge.
Preheat the oven to 150°C (gas mark 5).
Oil muffin tins with a brush and fill them about 3/4 full of batter.
Bake in the oven for about 20 to 25 minutes. The muffins are ready when the edge
comes off easily (be careful, they don't brown, so don't trust their color!).
Unmold the muffins as soon as they come out of the oven and
wrap them in cling film to keep them soft.
Enjoy!

Pragerplätzchen (Christmas shortbread with meringue)

Serves 6

Preparation time: 25 min

Ingredients

250g flour
250g butter
3 eggs
200g sugar (very fine powder or powdered sugar)
lemon zest
cinnamon
baking powder
raisins or chocolate chips

Preparation

These shortbreads are made of a shortbread base and a meringue preparation.

Remember to preheat your oven to 200°C (thermostat 6-7).
Dough:
Mix the flour, 2 tablespoons of sugar, lemon zest, cinnamon, yeast, butter, egg yolks.
Mix until you obtain a compact and homogeneous paste.
Meringue preparation (be careful, it should not become a hard meringue...):
Beat the 3 egg whites until stiff.
Carefully add 200 g of sugar (very fine, if possible powdered sugar)
Form small round shortbread with the dough, garnish them with the meringue preparation, add on each shortbread :
- a raisin
- a chocolate chip
- nothing (but it's less pretty)
Place in the oven and cook for 10 to 15 minutes at 175-200°C (thermostat 6-7). Be careful, meringues are delicate, watch them carefully!

Shortbreads or Scottish shortbread

Serves 6

Preparation time: 15 min

Ingredients

250g of flour
250g of semi-salted butter
125g of powdered sugar
125g of cornstarch

Preparation

Mix the softened butter and the powdered sugar.
Add the flour and the cornstarch.
The dough will first be powdered and then will gradually become homogeneous (do not add water!!!).
Roll out the dough to 1.5 cm thick and cut out with a cookie cutter (or coffee cup!).
Or simpler: make balls and crush them slightly...
Bake at 180°C for about 12 minutes, the shortbread should remain rather white (but it depends on your taste...).
Sprinkle with sugar after baking.
This recipe is easier with a mixer...

Christmas cookie simplissime

Serves 6

Preparation time: 15 min

Ingredients

250g flour
250g brown sugar

1/2 sachet of yeast
1/2 teaspoon of fine salt
1/2 teaspoon of ginger
1/2 teaspoon of nutmeg
1dl of milk
2dl oil
4 eggs
100g raisins soaked in half water / half rum
50g of chopped nuts
50g of chopped hazelnuts
3 cups of grated carrots

Preparation

Mix flour, brown sugar, yeast, salt, spices.
Add milk, oil, eggs. Mix again.
Add raisins, nuts, carrots.
Pour into a buttered cake tin.
Bake for about 1 hour at 200°C (if the cake gets too brown, put a piece of aluminum foil
on the top in the middle of the baking time). The cake should be golden brown.
Unmould when cold on a rack. Decorate with powdered sugar
and small Christmas decorations to your taste.

Spice cupcakes
Number of cakes: 20

Preparation time: 30 min

Ingredients

250g of flour
250g of sugar
100g melted butter
125g almond powder
2 eggs
1/2 teaspoon of salt
1 teaspoon cinnamon powder
1 teaspoon of allspice

Preparation

Turn on the oven to thermostat 6 (180°C).
Mix everything together. Knead by hand and shape into small balls. Place on a buttered
baking sheet, spacing them slightly apart. Put in the oven at half height.

Crunchy nut cookies
cookies: 20

Preparation time: 15 min

Ingredients

250g flour
2 eggs
150g of sugar
1/2 sachet of yeast
1 sachet of vanilla sugar
50g of soft butter

Preparation

Mix the butter, sugar and vanilla sugar until you get a homogeneous paste.
Add the eggs and mix well.
Mix the flour and the yeast and add them to the preparation, always making sure
to mix well in order to have a homogeneous paste without lumps.
Add the nuts before baking the cookies.
Preheat the oven to 180°C (gas mark 6).
Place the cookies on the baking sheet covered with baking paper and
make sure to space them out, as they may stick together.
Bake for 9 to 12 minutes and serve warm or cold.

Chocolate pine nut cookies
Serves 5

Preparation time: 20 min

Ingredients

250g of flour
2 eggs
200g of sugar
60g of butter
1 plain yogurt
1 sachet of baking powder
200g of pine nuts
100g of dark chocolate

Preparation

Mix the eggs with the sugar. Then add the butter, the yogurt,
and the flour mixed with the baking powder.
Break the chocolate into small pieces, and add them to the preparation. Add the pine nuts.
Divide the mixture between 5 small individual tart pans.
Bake for 10 to 15 minutes at 200°C (gas mark 6-7).
The cakes should be golden brown.

Flat muffins from Lili's mom (England)
muffins: 10

Preparation time: 10 min

Ingredients

250g of flour
30g of butter
10g sugar
5g of salt
1 sachet of baking powder
12.5cl of milk (a small glass)

Preparation

Preheat the oven to 200°C (thermostat 6-7).
Make a fountain in the flour, put the yeast, the softened butter, the salt, the sugar and the milk.
Mix into a smooth dough.
Roll out to a thickness of 1 cm, cut out rounds with a glass.
Put in a hot oven on a buttered plate for about 10 minutes.
They should remain white.
Cut in half, spread with butter, serve hot with tea for breakfast, brunch or in the afternoon.

Orange and chocolate madeleines
madeleines: 12

Preparation time: 15 min

Ingredients

250g flour
4 eggs
200g powdered sugar
180g of butter
2oranges
75g of chocolate
Powdered sugar
Salt

Preparation

Preheat your oven to 190°C (thermostat 6-7).
Butter and flour your madeleine mold.
In a bowl, sift the flour and salt.
In another bowl, beat the eggs and sugar with an electric mixer on medium
power until the mixture triples in volume.
Take the orange peels and set aside.

Add the flour mixture, melted butter, orange zest and chocolate chips to this mixture. Mix well.
Fill the moulds with 3/4 of the dough.
Bake the madeleines for 11 minutes. They should be golden and firm to the touch.
Wait 2 minutes to remove from the molds so they don't deflate.
Sprinkle with powdered sugar just before serving.

cyclops or chocolate shortbread
pieces: 6

Preparation time: 30 min

Ingredients

250g of flour
50g of almonds
125g of butter
70g of sugar
1 egg
2 tablespoons of cocoa
250g cooking chocolate
25cl of liquid cream
4 tablespoons of powdered sugar

Preparation

For the shortbread:
- Mix the softened butter with the sugar and almond powder, add the sifted flour little by little.
- Then add the egg to obtain a uniform dough (add a little water if the dough seems too dry) then the chocolate powder and keep in a cool place for at least 30 minutes.
For the ganache :
Heat the cream until it boils and pour it over the chocolate cut
into pieces. Leave to set for 5 minutes.
Return to the shortbread:
Roll out the dough to a maximum thickness of 4mm. It's a bit hard at first because the butter is cold but don't be discouraged, the shortbread dough always comes together!
Cut circles of about 10 cm in diameter with a pastry ring or a large tin can from which you will have removed the 2 bottoms with the can opener.
In half of the circles, cut smaller circles with a cupcake cutter.
Bake for 20 minutes at 180°.
In the meantime, mix the cream with the chocolate to obtain a thick liquid and chill.
When the rounds are cooked and cooled, and the ganache is thick, spread
the ganache generously on the rounds, sprinkle the circles with powdered
sugar and place a circle with ganache on top of a hole ....
It's even better the next day when the ganache has soaked the shortbread a little!

Dairy-free shortbread, coconut-light
Serves 6

Preparation time: 25 min

Ingredients

250g of flour
50g of grated coconut
150g of coconut oil
1 pinch of salt
3 tablespoons of sugar
4 egg yolks
Water to adjust the texture

Preparation

Preheat your oven to 200°C (gas mark 6-7).
If it is frozen, melt your coconut oil, just enough to make it liquid. Do not let
it heat too long to avoid cooking the eggs when incorporated.
Meanwhile, mix the dry goods (flour, shredded coconut, salt and sugar) in a
pot on one side, and prepare your egg yolks in another container.
Pour the melted coconut oil over the egg yolks and mix.
Make a well in your dry mixture. Stir in half of the coconut oil-egg yolk mixture
and mix once with a wooden spoon.
Then add the rest of the liquid mixture, first with a spoon, then by kneading by hand until
you have a smooth, soft, barely crumbly dough. Adjust the texture by moistening your
fingers with water while kneading. When the dough ball holds together, you're there.
Flour your work surface and rolling pin. Roll out the dough to the thickness that suits you (it
depends on your taste, I like them thick), cut out the whole dough with a cookie cutter.
The shortbread will bake for 10 minutes on a rack covered with parchment paper. They are ready
when the edges start to brown. The cooking time will depend on the thickness of your shortbread.
Once out of the oven, dry your shortbread flat on a rack until completely cool.
Enjoy! Can you feel that little taste of going back to your roots?

Melting cookies with chocolate chips
cookies: 15

Preparation time: 15 min

Ingredients

250g flour
50g almond powder
1 egg
150g of sugar
1/2 sachet of yeast
1 packet of vanilla sugar (or extract)
125g of butter
Chocolate

Preparation

Mix the butter, the sugar and the vanilla sugar (or a few drops of the extract)
until you get a homogeneous paste.
Add the egg and mix well.
Mix the flour, baking powder and almond powder and add to the mixture, making
sure to mix well to obtain a homogeneous paste without lumps.
Add the chocolate chips and mix well.
Personally, once the dough is ready, I spread it on a sheet of baking paper and roll it up
like a big candy so that I already have the shape of the cookies and I only have to cut
the dough into slices of 3 cm thickness once I put it in the fridge for 20 minutes.
Preheat the oven to 180°C (gas mark 6).
Place the cookies on the baking sheet covered with baking paper
and make sure to space them out as they will melt.
Bake for 9 to 11 minutes and serve warm.
Enjoy!

Weirdest, funkiest muffins ever: coconut and Turkish delight
muffins: 12

Preparation time: 20 min

Ingredients

250g flour
50g sugar
50g of coconut (I added 2-3 tablespoons in addition to the 50g)
12roses
1 sachet of yeast
1 egg
5cl of oil
25cl of milk
Grated coconut to sprinkle on top of the muffins

Preparation

In a bowl, mix the flour, the sugar, the coconut, the loukoums cut in small
pieces (use a pair of scissors soaked in hot water) and the yeast.
In another bowl, beat the egg, then add the oil and milk. Mix well.
Add this mixture to the flour bowl, mixing just a little to combine the ingredients.
Place in a muffin tin and sprinkle the top with coconut.
Bake for 20-25 min at 200°C.
Wait a day or two before eating, keeping them in an airtight box until then.

Hazelnut and 3 chocolate cookies
pieces: 12

Preparation time: 20 min

Ingredients

250g flour
75g of brown sugar
1 teaspoon of yeast
1 egg
100g of butter
25g oil
50g white chocolate
50g of dark chocolate
50g of milk chocolate
50g of hazelnuts
1 pinch of salt

Preparation

Preheat the oven to 200°C (thermostat 6-7). Coarsely crush the hazelnuts and the chocolate chips.
Melt the butter. Mix in the oil and the egg.
Mix the flour with the yeast, sugar and pinch of salt.
Stir the liquids into the flour and mix until a dough forms. Add the chocolate chips and hazelnuts.
Using an ice cream scoop, scoop out balls of dough and place on a baking
sheet lined with baking paper.
Bake in the oven for 9 minutes. When removed from the oven, the
cookies should still be soft, they will harden in the air.

Speculoos and berry muffins
muffins: 24

Preparation time: 15 min

Ingredients

250g flour
75g sugar
1 pinch of salt
1 packet of baking powder
1 egg
60g of butter
1 tablespoon of honey
30cl of milk
1 small bowl of frozen red fruit
10speculoos

Preparation

Preheat your oven to 180°C (thermostat 6)
Mix the flour, sugar, pinch of salt and the packet of baking powder in a large dish
Melt the butter
In another dish, mix the egg and the butter, and add the milk and the tablespoon of honey
Then pour this mixture little by little into the dish containing the flour. Stir

well to have a homogeneous paste, but it should not be too liquid
Crush the speculoos in a bowl to get very small pieces (keep some bigger
ones for decoration if you wish)
Take 24 paper cake tins (if possible insert them in a silicone mould so that the
muffins rise higher), and pour a tablespoon of batter into them
Now add a few pieces of speculoos or red fruits (or both)
Add more batter until it is halfway up the paper pan
On top, place a few more pieces of speculoos or berries
Bake for 20 minutes.

Soft honey and nut cookies
cookies: 25

Preparation time: 15 min

Ingredients

250g of flour
80g of sugar
80g of brown sugar
1 sachet of yeast
150g of walnuts
50g hazelnut powder
2 large tablespoons of liquid honey
125g melted butter
2 eggs

Preparation

Preheat the oven to 200°c.
Mix the flour, the sugars, the yeast, the hazelnut powder and the chopped walnuts.
Add the honey and sand the mixture (a bit like for a crumble).
Beat the eggs and melted butter; add them to the preparation
and mix until you obtain a compact dough.
Form small balls the size of a large walnut (if they stick to your fingers,
feel free to put a little flour on your hands).
Place the slightly crushed balls on a baking sheet, well spaced out.
Bake the cookies for 5 to 10 minutes until they are a nice golden color.
The cookies can be stored for 3 days in an airtight box.

Lebkuchen (traditional German cookies)
Cookies: 30

Preparation time: 15 min

Ingredients

250g flour
85g almond powder

1 teaspoon of yeast
1/2 teaspoon of bicarbonate
1 pinch of clove powder
1 pinch of nutmeg powder
1 pinch ground black pepper
2 teaspoons ginger powder
1 teaspoon cinnamon powder
85g of butter
20cl liquid honey
lemon peel

Preparation

In a large bowl, mix the flour, almonds, baking powder, baking soda, spices and herbs. In a saucepan over low heat, melt the honey with the butter, then pour the mixture into the bowl. Add the lemon zest and mix until you have a firm paste. Cover and let cool. Preheat oven to 180°C (gas mark 6) and line two baking sheets with parchment paper. Shape 30 balls of dough, then flatten them slightly and place them on the baking sheets, spacing them well. Bake for 15 minutes, then cool on a rack. Beat the egg white, then mix it with the powdered sugar and water until you have a smooth glaze. Dip the top of each cookie into the glaze. Let dry in a warm place.

Light Lemon Cookies

pieces: 40

Preparation time: 20 min

Ingredients

250g flour
8g of aspartame
1 level teaspoon of baking powder
salt
vanilla bean
1 egg yolk
Lemon
10cl of white cheese0% (or fromage blanc)
50g of butter

Preparation

Sift the flour, aspartame and baking powder. Add a pinch of salt, the vanilla, the egg yolk, a little lemon juice (or zest according to taste), the cottage cheese and the soft butter. Mix well, form a ball of dough and chill for 30 minutes. Preheat your oven to 180°C (thermostat 6) Roll out the dough on a floured surface and cut out shapes with a cookie cutter. Bake for 10 min then let cool. Mix 2 tablespoons of aspartame with a little lemon and brush the surface of the shortbread.

Original American Cookies with Companion
cookies: 15

Preparation time: 15 min

Ingredients

250g flour
90g brown sugar
100g chocolate chips
125g of butter
1 egg
1 sachet of vanilla sugar
2 teaspoons of liquid honey
1/2 sachet of yeast
1 pinch of salt

Preparation

Preheat the oven to 220 °C (th. 7-8).
Put the butter in the bowl of your Companion, then melt it with
the mixer knife / speed 3 / 40 °C / 5 min.
Add the salt, egg and honey, then beat with the mixer knife / speed 6 / 0 °C / 15 sec.
Add the flour, sugars and yeast and beat again with the mixer knife / speed 6 / 0 °C / 25 sec.
Add half the chocolate chips and mix gently with the dough cutter / speed 3 / 0 °C / 25 sec.
Remove the cookie dough from the bowl, then shape it into balls using an ice
cream scoop. Place them on a baking sheet lined with parchment paper, then add
a few sprinkles on top. Press them down lightly with your fingertips.
Bake for 9 to 11 minutes, depending on your texture preference.

Original American Cookies in Cookeo
cookies: 15

Preparation time: 15 min

Ingredients

250g flour
90g brown sugar
100g chocolate chips
125g of butter
1 egg
1 sachet of vanilla sugar
2 teaspoons of liquid honey
1/2 sachet of yeast
1 pinch of salt

Preparation

Preheat the oven to 220 °C (th. 7-8).
Put the butter in the tank of your Cookeo, then melt it.
Add the salt, the egg and the honey, then beat.
Pour in the flour, sugars and yeast and beat again.
Add half the chocolate chips and mix gently.
Take the cookie dough out of the bowl and shape it into balls with an ice cream scoop. Place them on a parchment-lined baking sheet, then add a few sprinkles to the top. Press them down lightly with your fingertips.
Bake for 9 to 11 minutes, depending on your texture preference.

Original American Cookies in Thermomix
cookies: 15

Preparation time: 15 min

Ingredients

250g flour
90g brown sugar
100g chocolate chips
125g of butter
1 egg
1 sachet of vanilla sugar
2 teaspoons of liquid honey
1/2 sachet of baking powder
1 pinch of salt

Preparation

Preheat the oven to 220 °C (th. 7-8).
Put the butter in the bowl of your food processor, then melt it for 5 min / 40 °C / speed 4.
Add the salt, egg and honey, then beat for 15 sec / 0 °C / vit.6.
Add the flour, sugars and yeast and beat again for 25 sec / 0 °C / vit.6.
Add half of the chocolate chips, then mix gently for 25 sec / 0 °C / spoon speed / reverse.
Remove the cookie dough from the bowl and shape it into balls using an ice cream scoop. Place them on a baking sheet lined with parchment paper, then add a few sprinkles on top. Press them down lightly with your fingertips.
Bake for 9 to 11 minutes, depending on your texture preference.

Original American Cookies at Cooking Chef
cookies: 15

Preparation Time: 15 min

Ingredients

250g flour
90g brown sugar

100g chocolate chips
125g of butter
1 egg
1 sachet of vanilla sugar
2 teaspoons of liquid honey
1/2 sachet of yeast
1 pinch of salt

Preparation

Preheat the oven to 220 °C (th. 7-8).
Put the butter in the bowl of your Cooking Chef, then melt it
with the mixer tool / 5 min / 40 °C / speed 4.
Add the salt, egg and honey, then beat with the mixer tool / 15 sec / 0 °C / speed 7.
Add the flour, sugars and yeast and beat again with the mixer / 25 sec / 0 °C / speed 7.
Add half the chocolate chips and mix gently with the mixer tool / 25 sec / 0 °C / speed 2.
Remove the cookie dough from the bowl and shape into balls using an ice cream
scoop. Place them on a baking sheet lined with parchment paper, then add a
few sprinkles on top. Press them down lightly with your fingertips.
Bake for 9 to 11 minutes, depending on your texture preference.

Original American Cookies at Monsieur Cuisine
cookies: 15

Preparation Time: 15 min

Ingredients

250g flour
90g brown sugar
100g chocolate chips
125g of butter
1 egg
1 sachet of vanilla sugar
2 teaspoons of liquid honey
1/2 sachet of yeast
1 pinch of salt

Preparation

Preheat the oven to 220°C (th. 7-8).
Put the butter in the bowl of your Mister Cuisine and melt it.
Add the salt, egg and honey and beat.
Add the flour, sugars and yeast and beat again.
Add half the chocolate chips and mix gently.
Take the cookie dough out of the bowl and shape it into balls with an ice
cream scoop. Place them on a parchment-lined baking sheet, then add a few
sprinkles to the top. Press them down lightly with your fingertips.

Bake for 9 to 11 minutes, depending on your texture preference.

Spider Cookie

pieces: 15

Preparation Time: 15 min

Ingredients

250g flour
90g of canneroux sugar (or brown sugar)
1 sachet of vanilla sugar
1 pinch of salt
1/2 sachet of yeast
1 egg
125g of soft butter
2 teaspoons of honey
Chocolate (to taste)

Preparation

Mix the flour, sugars, salt and yeast in a large bowl.
Melt the butter and add the beaten egg and the 2 spoonfuls of honey to the mixture.
Add the chocolate chips (preferably milk chocolate, but I've tasted 3 chocolate cookies before and they're delicious), and mix with a wooden spoon.
Preheat your oven to 220°C (gas mark 7-8), with the rack on low.
Shape cookies about 10 cm in diameter and place them on a baking sheet. They should be fairly spaced out.
Put them in the oven for 9 to 11 minutes, depending on whether you want them to be extra soft, chewy or crunchy...
Decorate the cookies.
Melt the chocolate.
Place the melted chocolate in a piping bag and draw on each cookie the dough of the spiders.
Place 2 chocolate balls on top of the cookies.
On one of the two balls, stick 2 half Dragibus® to form the eyes.

Cookie Fries

Serves: 6

Preparation time: 20 min

Ingredients

250g of flour
90g of brown sugar
1 egg
125g of butter
2 teaspoons of honey

Chocolate
1 pinch of salt
1/2 sachet of yeast
Frying oil

Preparation

Mix flour, sugar, honey, salt and yeast.
Add the soft butter and the egg. Mix well with a wooden spoon.
Add the chocolate chips and work the mixture with your hands.
Roll out the dough on a sheet of parchment paper or a lightly floured work surface.
Cut the dough into strips and then cut the strips into fries.
Dip the cookie fries in hot oil for 1 or 2 minutes and place on paper towels.

Turnips of Marseille (St Victor)
turnips: 8

Preparation time: 15 min

Ingredients

250g of flour
90sugar
20ml olive oil (1,5 cs)
45ml of orange blossom
1 egg
1 pinch of salt

Preparation

Whisk together powdered sugar and egg in a bowl.
Mix until creamy.
Add olive oil, orange blossom water and salt. Mix again.
Add the flour. Mix with a spatula and then by hand until you have a smooth dough.
Flour the work surface. Roll out the dough into sausage-like shapes 2 cm thick and 15 cm long.
Place the rolls on a baking sheet with parchment paper.
Flatten the ends of the sausages and crack the middle of the sausages with a blade.
Brush each navette with orange blossom water. Bake in the oven. Bake in 3
stages: 15 min at 165°C, 8 min at 150°C and 2 min on the grill.

Norwegian omelette with pink cookies from Reims
people: 8

Preparation time: 1h45

Ingredients

250g of wheat flour
250g of powdered sugar

125g of butter + 20g for the mold
6 eggs
1 sachet of vanilla sugar
Kirsch

Preparation

Start by preparing the sponge cake:
Preheat the oven to 180°C (gas mark 6).
Heat a pan of water and place a container in it to make a bain-marie.
Put the powdered sugar and eggs in the water bath. Whisk vigorously
until the mixture becomes frothy and forms a ribbon.
Remove from the water bath and add the flour and vanilla
sugar. Mix well and add the melted butter.
Mix, the dough should be smooth. Butter a cake tin, pour in the batter and bake for 35 minutes.
Turn out.
Let cool.
Cut in the sponge cake lengthwise to get two nice slices of about 0.5 cm thick.
Soak the slices of sponge cake with kirsch, possibly diluted with water to attenuate
the taste of alcohol.
- Ice:
Using a peeler, cut shavings from the white chocolate.
Finely grind the pink cookies in a blender.
Blanch the egg yolks with the powdered sugar in an electric mixer. The mixture
should be frothy and a bit thick.
Still using an electric mixer, whip the cream until very stiff (advice: the cream must be very
cold; whipping the cream in two 250g steps is easier than whipping the 500g directly).
Gently fold the whipped cream into the whitened eggs.
Beat the egg whites until stiff and gently fold them into the egg-whipped
cream-sugar mixture until the mixture is well blended.
Divide the mixture in two.
In one, add the white chocolate shavings.
In the other, add the pink cookie powder.
- Arrange the ice cream:
In the same mold that was used to bake the sponge cake, pour the white chocolate mixture.
Place a slice of sponge cake on top (this slice of sponge cake can be replaced
by a layer of coarsely crushed meringues).
Then pour the pink cookie mixture.
Cover with a slice of sponge cake (if the sponge cake does not completely cover the
surface of the ice cream, adjust with other pieces of soaked sponge cake).
Place overnight in the freezer.
- The next day:
Beat the egg whites until stiff for the meringue. Once the whites are stiff,
add the powdered sugar and beat again to combine the sugar.
Turn out of the mould, if necessary rinsing the sides of the mould with lukewarm water.
Place the omelet on a baking dish (the bottom being a slice of sponge

cake and the top the white chocolate ice cream).
Cover the omelet with a layer of meringue and decorate with the remaining meringue using a piping bag.
Optional: decorate with red candied fruit or Reims croquignoles.
Place under the broiler until the meringue is lightly browned.
Place in the freezer at least 3-4 hours before serving.
Just before serving, flambé the kirsch ice cream in front of your guests!

Cantoches Raspberry Maxi Muffins
Serves 8

Preparation time: 20 min

Ingredients

250g wheat or rice flour
3 eggs
125g of salted butter
150ml cow or soy milk
100g sugar according to the fruit used (raspberries = 125g)
1 sachet of baking powder with or without gluten
1 pinch of salt
25g of dark chocolate from which to cut out large chips

Preparation

Start by taking the butter out of the fridge (30 minutes before is better)! Preheat the oven to 210°C.(thermostat7)
Butter and flour the moulds unless you have silicone ones.
Mix the flour, baking powder and salt in a large bowl.
In a bowl, work the butter into a creamy consistency with your hands. Add the sugar, still mixing with your hands. Add and whisk in the eggs, taking care to incorporate them well. Then add the flour/yeast/salt mixture to the bowl little by little while continuing to whisk. Finally, add the fruit, in this case raspberries (fresh in summer or frozen in winter). On a board, cut out chocolate chips from your 30gr chocolate bar and add them to the dough.
Bake each round for 15 to 25 minutes at 210°C.

Breton cookies
cookies: 30

Preparation time: 10 min

Ingredients

250g buckwheat flour + for spreading
100g brown sugar
5cl of oil
7cl of cidredoux
1 good pinch of salt

Preparation

Put the flour in a bowl.
Pour the sugar, salt, oil and cider in the middle.
Knead with an electric whisk (dough hooks) until the dough becomes
smooth and supple, without sticking to your fingers.
Roll into a ball, wrap in plastic wrap, and let firm up for at least 30 minutes in the refrigerator.
Generously flour the work surface.
Roll out the dough to a thickness of about 4 mm.
Cut out with a cookie cutter or use a baby jar or an upside down glass to cut into 3-4 cm disks.
Line a baking sheet. Carefully place the discs on top.
Place in a conventional oven preheated to 210°C (gas mark 7) and bake for 10 minutes.
Take the cookies out when they are still soft and let them cool on a rack, they will harden.

Gluten and lactose free muffins
Muffins: 9

Preparation time: 15 min

Ingredients

250g gluten free flour
30g cornstarch
100g powdered sugar
150ml almond drink
2 eggs
8 tablespoons of oil (4 oils for me)
1 sachet of vanilla sugar
1 sachet of gluten free baking powder
1 pinch of salt
Orange marmalade

Preparation

Heat the oven (for me, 180°C, thermostat 6).
In a bowl, mix the powders:
Flour, cornstarch, sugar, vanilla sugar, baking powder, salt.
In a second bowl, mix the liquids:
Almond drink, eggs, oil.
Put the preparation 2 in the bowl 1 by mixing delicately (no whisk, the wooden spoon is enough).
Using a tablespoon, put a dose of batter in each mold. Then with a teaspoon,
put a dose of marmalade on top.
Close by placing a small amount of dough with the tablespoon again.
Bake for about 30 minutes.

Small cakes 'suze
Serves: 6

Preparation time: 5 min

Ingredients

250g of white flour
1 sachet of vanilla sugar
1 sachet of Alsatian yeast
3 tablespoons of orange blossom water
10cl of hot coffee

Preparation

In the bowl of a food processor, mix the powders and the orange blossom water.
Gradually add the hot coffee until you obtain a creamy cake batter.
Fill a piping bag with this dough and form small cakes on a baking
sheet or a sheet of parchment paper.
Bake for about 20 minutes at 170°C (gas mark 5-6).

Shortbread with 3 seeds
shortbread: 60

Preparation time: 20 min

Ingredients

250g of flourT80
1 sachet of baking powder
1 pinch of salt
150g of cane sugar
30g sunflower seeds
30g of sesame seeds
30g poppy seeds
150g soft butter, softened
2 spoons of almond puree (optional)
1 egg

Preparation

Using a food processor fitted with a mixer or by hand in a large bowl, gradually mix all
the ingredients in the order indicated above, mixing well between each ingredient.
Microwave the butter for about 50 seconds to soften it.
If you are using a food processor with a mixer, you will need to finish kneading the dough by hand.
Once all the ingredients are mixed, you should obtain a compact and homogeneous
ball, a little crumbly but smooth when pressed on the edges of the bowl. Preheat
your oven to 150°C (fan oven).
Make one or more dough balls with a diameter of 2 to 3cm maximum. Then cut slices of
1cm maximum width that you will lay out on a baking sheet provided with parchment
paper. It is not normally necessary to refrigerate the puffs before cutting them. The
palets will tend to crush a little when cut, so give them a round shape by hand before

placing them on the baking sheet. To ensure that the shortbread does not touch each other during baking, be sure to space the shortbread 2 cm apart in staggered rows. Place your tray in the oven and cook for 15 to 20 minutes. I usually make three batches of about 20 shortbread each. If you have several trays you can put them all in the oven at the same time on different levels. Check the baking time. For soft shortbread, it should barely brown and remain light. For crunchy shortbread, they should be cooked for a good 20 minutes until they are golden brown. Let cool before tasting. Consume with a tea, an infusion or a coffee. If you can wait until then...

Mantecaos with cinnamon (Moroccan cookies)

people: 4

Preparation time: 10 min

Ingredients

250g of sifted flour
1dl of oil
125g of sugar
lemon zest
Cinnamon powder

Preparation

Put the flour in a jar and dig a well. Add the oil, sugar and lemon peel. Mix everything together.
Butter and flour a baking sheet.
Form balls of dough slightly flattened.
Put them on the plate and let rest 20 minutes.
Preheat oven to 200°C.
Sprinkle the cakes with cinnamon to taste. Put in the oven for 20 minutes.

Easy strawberry cookie glasses

Serves: 6

Preparation time: 15 min

Ingredients

250g of strawberries
1 jar of cottage cheese
60g of powdered sugar
1 box of cookies

Preparation

Wash, cut your strawberries in small pieces, and sweeten them. Sweeten the cottage cheese to your liking. Break the cookies into small pieces.
In verrines, put a layer of strawberries, a layer of cottage cheese, a few pieces of cookies and then repeat, finishing with a few pieces of strawberries or cookies for decoration.
Chill for 1 hour and enjoy.

Strawberry and madeleine verrines
Serves 8

Preparation time: 20 min

Ingredients

250g of strawberries
250g of mascarpone
100g of powdered sugar
3 eggs
12madeleines

Preparation

Cut the hulled strawberries into pieces (keep some whole for decoration).
Separate the egg whites from the yolks.
Beat the egg whites until stiff.
In a bowl, mix the mascarpone with the egg yolks and sugar.
Incorporate the egg whites into the preparation.
In the bottom of the verrines, crumble the madeleines then cover with the preparation and strawberries then again with madeleines. Finish with a layer of mascarpone cream.
Set aside in a cool place for at least 3 hours.
Just before serving, decorate the verrines with strawberries. You
can add a coulis if you wish. Serve chilled.

Strawberry and macaroon tiramisu
Serves 4

Preparation time: 15 min

Ingredients

250g of strawberries
250g of mascarpone
125g of powdered sugar
3 eggs
8 raspberry macaroons
tagada® strawberries (candy)

Preparation

Cut strawberries into small cubes and mix with 50g of sugar.
Beat the egg yolks with the remaining sugar until they are white. Add the mascarpone and the beaten egg whites.
Melt the Tagada ® strawberries in a saucepan with a little water (keep some for decoration).
Place a layer of strawberries, two broken macaroons, Tagada ® syrup in a glass and finish with a thick layer of mascarpone/egg/sugar mixture. Decorate with the remaining Tagada ® strawberries.

Set aside in a cool place for at least 4 hours before serving...

Strawberries and Brittany palets in a pan
people: 4

Preparation time: 10 min

Ingredients

250g of strawberries
8 palets bretons
20cl of fresh cream (optional)
2 tablespoons brown sugar
half a lemon juice.

Preparation

Wash and hull the strawberries. Cut them into pieces and set them aside in a plate. Coarsely crumble 6 palets bretons over a bowl. Melt the sugar with the juice of the half lime over low heat in a frying pan. Pour in the strawberries and gently mix them with a spoon to coat them well. Let them cool for 2 minutes, stirring all the time...Place all the crumbled palets on the bottom of 4 ramekins and spread the warm strawberries on top...Break the remaining palets into pieces and place them between the strawberries...If you are greedy, serve with fresh cream.

Strawberry Financiers
pieces: 24

Preparation time: 15 min

Ingredients

250g of frozen strawberries
6 egg whites
200g of butter
80g of flour
200g powdered sugar
80g almond powder

Preparation

Heat the oven to 180°C (thermostat 6).
Melt the butter and let it cool.
Whip the egg whites lightly with a whisk.
Add the powdered sugar, mix, add the almond powder and the flour, mix, add the warmed butter.
Mix well.
Fill the moulds 3/4 of the way with the mixture (butter and flour them if they are not made of silicone).
Place 1 or 2 strawberries (depending on their size) in each mold.
Bake for 15 minutes.
Turn out of the oven and serve warm or cold.

Shortbread Cake
Serves 8

Preparation time: 40 min

Ingredients

250g of shortbread cakes
125g butter
150g of sugar
3 eggs
25cl of coffee

Preparation

Beat the butter and the sugar to obtain a homogeneous paste.
Mix in the 3 egg yolks and one egg white.
Quickly dip the cakes one by one in the cold coffee and arrange them on a plate
(the best way is to make a kind of flower, with a cake in the center and the
others around), then with a knife spread a thin layer of cream on top.
Repeat the operation until the end of the cookies. For the last layer, cover the sides.
Leave in the fridge for 8 hours or overnight.

Redcurrant cakes
cakes: 12

Preparation time: 15 min

Ingredients

250g of currants
4 egg whites
100g almond powder
2 tablespoons of flour
150g of caster sugar

Preparation

Preheat the oven to thermostat 6 (180°C).
Pour the almond powder and the flour in a bowl and mix.
Beat the eggs until stiff and add the sugar little by little while continuing to beat
the eggs. Gently add the almond/flour mixture. Add the currants.
Butter small molds. Spread the preparation in the moulds and cook approximately
25mn. The little cakes should take a small blond tint.
Turn out and sprinkle with powdered sugar.

Tiramisu with red fruits and speculoos
Serves 6

Preparation time: 20 min

Ingredients

250g of mascarpone
100g sugar
3 eggs
16 peculiar cookies
300g frozen red fruit

Preparation

Defrost the red fruits.
In a bowl, crush the speculoos.
Prepare the eggs.
Separate the whites and beat them until stiff.
Beat the yolks with the sugar until the mixture turns white.
Add the mascarpone to the egg yolk + sugar mixture and mix until smooth.
Add the egg whites to the previous mixture with delicacy.
Put a layer of speculoos in verrines, followed by the mascarpone mousse and the red fruits.
Put back in the fridge and serve well chilled.

Verrine mascarpone speculoos pineapple
Serves 6

Preparation time: 20 min

Ingredients

250g of mascarpone
10speculoos
4 eggs
6 tablespoons of sugar
6 pineapple rings

Preparation

Separate the whites from the yolks.
Mix the mascarpone with the yolks and sugar. Beat the egg whites
until stiff. Gently add them to the preparation.
Put 1 crumbled speculoos in the bottom of a glass, add a little mascarpone, put some
pineapple pieces then mascarpone, finish with crumbled speculoos just before serving.
Chill for at least 3 hours.

Small glasses of mascarpone ricotta with speculoos and stewed red fruits
Serves 6

Preparation time: 1 hour

Ingredients

250g of mascarpone
125g of ricotta cheese
2 eggs
60g of sugar

Preparation

Put the fruit in a saucepan, add the sugar.
Bring to the boil, reduce the heat and cook for 30 minutes.
Remove from heat and add gelatin.
Let cool completely.
In a dish, whiten the yolks with the sugar.
Add ricotta cheese and mix well.
Add mascarpone, mix again.
Beat the egg whites until stiff (add a pinch of salt).
Gently add the whites to the mixture.
In glasses:
Place one or two spoonfuls of fruit.
Cover with pieces of speculoos.
Put a layer of cream.
Top with speculoos.
Add more fruit.
Finish with a few pieces of speculoos.

Tiramisu with speculoos (without eggs)
Serves 6

Preparation time: 15 min

Ingredients

250g of mascarpone
1 vanilla bean (optional)
500g of speculoos
1bol of caféfort
30g sugar (vanilla or not)
2 whipped cream (50 cl in all)
Bitter or non-bitter cocoa for topping

Preparation

Start by making the coffee so that it has time to cool down while you make the cream.
Mix the mascarpone with a vanilla bean (which I use to replace the egg yolks while giving a
vanilla note), and 30 gr of sugar. (Don't forget that speculoos is an extremely sweet cake!)
Once the mixture is homogeneous, add in several times the whipped
cream bombs (or the one you made at home is even better).
Don't stir your whipped cream like crazy.
Lift the cream with your whisk and very gently fold in the mousse. This is a

crucial step to have a good foamy cream and not a floating island!
Once the cream is finished, divide it in half to have an equal amount
for each layer. (For my part I managed to make 3 layers).
Take your dessert dish, and start the first layer of speculoos dipped in
cold coffee (just in and out. Don't linger in the bowl).
Once the layer is finished, put the first layer of cream gently, then sprinkle with
bitter (or non-bitter) cocoa. And repeat the step until you run out of cream.
Finish with the cocoa dusting, film and leave in the fridge for several hours.
Ideally overnight!

Tiramisu nutella speculoos

Serves: 4

Preparation time: 25 min

Ingredients

250g of mascarpone
200g of nutella
150g of speculoos
30g powdered sugar
2 eggs
10cl of milk
1 tablespoon vanilla liquid (or a bag of vanilla sugar)
2 tablespoons of chocolate powder (preferably bitter)

Preparation

Take the eggs and separate the yolks from the whites.
Beat the yolks with the vanilla, sugar and mascarpone. Whisk until the mixture
is smooth and creamy.
Beat the egg whites with a pinch of salt. Fold them in very gently with the
mascarpone cream and mix very gently so as not to break the egg whites.
Melt the nutella with the milk in the microwave or in a saucepan.
Break the speculoos into pieces and place them in the bottom of each glass.
Crumble them with a spatula or the end of a rolling pin, for example.
Cover the speculoos with melted nutella. Add the mascarpone mousse on top.
Top with crumbled speculoos and/or chocolate powder.
Place the verrines in the refrigerator for a minimum of 4 hours and
at best overnight to allow the tiramisu mousse to set.

strawberry and speculoos verrine

Serves 6

Preparation time: 15 min

Ingredients

250g of mascarpone

250g strawberries
8speculoos
50g powdered sugar
4 teaspoons of caramelliquide
1 egg white
Cinnamon powder

Preparation

Crush the speculoos into small pieces and mix with the mascarpone. Add the sugar and mix again. Wash and hull the strawberries, cut them into very small cubes and keep in a cool place. Whip the egg whites until stiff and cook them in boiling water and vinegar to obtain 6 small balls (like floating islands).
Then assemble the verrines: at the bottom, divide the speculoos and mascarpone mixture into six verrines and then divide the strawberries into small cubes on top.
Pour a teaspoon of liquid caramel and finish with the egg ball.
Sprinkle with a little cinnamon and put in the refrigerator for about 20 minutes so that the cream sets well. It's ready to be served with a chouquette.

Easy Tiramisu with pink cookies from Reims
Serves 6

Preparation time: 25 min

Ingredients

250g of mascarpone
25cl of fresh cream
5 eggs
50g of powdered sugar
12 Reims rose cookies
1 tablespoon of sugar

Preparation

Start by separating the egg whites and yolks.
Mix the powdered sugar and the egg yolks until the mixture becomes foamy.
Add the mascarpone and cream to the mixture. Beat the egg whites until stiff.
Gently fold the whites into the mixture.
In a dish, start with a layer of pink cookies, then put a layer of the mixture, then a layer of pink cookies and finish with a layer of the mixture.
Sprinkle with pink cookie crumbs.
Set aside in the refrigerator for 1 hour before enjoying!

Very easy chocolate speculoos tiramisu
Serves 4

Preparation time: 15 min

Ingredients

250g of mascarpone
2 eggs
60g sugar
60g dark chocolate
60g of speculoos

Preparation

Separate the whites from the yolks.
Mix the yolks with the sugar until the mixture turns white then add the mascarpone.
Beat the egg whites until stiff and gently combine the two preparations.
Separate the preparation into 2 parts.
Melt the chocolate in a double boiler and add it to one of the two preparations.
Place pieces of speculoos in the bottom of the verrines or dish.
Cover with the chocolate mixture and then with the plain mixture.
Cover to the top of the verrines or dish.
Sprinkle with speculoos crumbs and refrigerate for 24 hours.

Lemon-Speculoos Wedding Tiramisu
Serves 5

Preparation time: 15 min

Ingredients

250g of mascarpone
3 tablespoons of powdered sugar
3 eggs
1 egg yolk
1 yellow lemon
1 lime
60g of coconut powder
1 pinch of salt
20peculos cookies
1 cup of coffee

Preparation

Whisk the egg yolks with the powdered sugar. Once this mixture is whitened, add
the mascarpone and stir until smooth (use an electric mixer if necessary).
Add the juice of the two lemons, as well as the zest of the yellow
lemon, and the coconut powder. Mix well.
Beat the egg whites with a pinch of salt. Add them to the previous mixture,
stirring gently so as not to break the whites. Set aside.
In each individual ramekin, place two speculos quickly dipped in coffee in the bottom.
Pour a good layer of mascarpone mixture on top. Do the same for each ramekin.

Chill for at least 2 hours before serving.
Just before serving, you can decorate your desserts by sprinkling the mascarpone mousse with specula crumbs, lemon zest, coconut powder, chocolate chips... Let your imagination run wild!

Tiramisu speculoos granny smith

Serves 4

Preparation time: 30 min

Ingredients

250g of mascarpone
3eggs
60sugar
1granny smith
15speculoos

Preparation

Put the sugar in a bowl.
Separate the egg whites from the yolks, mix the yolks with the sugar.
Put the whites in another bowl and beat them until they are stiff.
Add the mascarpone to the sugar-egg mixture and mix vigorously.
Gently fold the whites into the mixture with a spatula.
Put the preparation in a cool place.
Wash and core the apples, cut them into small cubes, put them in a
bowl and sprinkle them with a little lemon juice.
Crush the speculoos.
Remove the mixture from the refrigerator.
Remove from the containers (glasses, verrines,...).
Place a base of speculoos in the bottom of the glass, then a small layer of apple,
then a little of the mixture, then a new layer of speculoos and apple.
Pour more of the mixture and finish with a few diced granny
apples and a few pieces of crushed speculoos.

Sweetened glasses with pink cookies

Serves 8

Preparation time: 20 min

Ingredients

250g of mascarpone
3 eggs
80g of sugar
10 Reims rose cookies
25cl of coffee
salt

Preparation

Take the mascarpone out of the refrigerator 15 minutes before you start the preparation, it will be more malleable.
In a bowl: separate the egg whites from the yolks. Add a pinch of salt to make it easier to beat the egg whites. Set aside.
In a bowl: whisk the mascarpone with the yolks, then add the sugar.
Gently fold in the egg whites to obtain a smooth cream.
Break 4 Reims cookies in half, soak each piece in the warm coffee and line the bottom of the verrines.
Coat the pink cookies with the mascarpone mixture. Chill for at least 4 hours before serving.
Crush the remaining cookies into coarse crumbs and sprinkle over the top.
Enjoy, it's delicious!

Lemon speculoos cream

Serves 6

Preparation time: 20 min

Ingredients

250g of mascarpone
3 organic eggs
1 pack of speculoos
85g of sugar
1 organic lemon

Preparation

Separate the whites from the yolks of your eggs. Keep them.
In a saucepan, beat the yolks with the sugar. Incorporate the mascarpone. Make zests with the peel and add them with the juice of your whole lemon.
Beat the eggs until stiff and mix them gently into the mixture.
Crumble the speculoos into a bowl. Prepare your verrines with a layer of speculoos followed by a layer of lemon cream. Repeat the operation.
Keep in the fridge for an hour and enjoy!

Tiramisu verrines with red fruits and macaroons

Serves: 4

Preparation time: 10 min

Ingredients

250g of mascarpone
3 fresh eggs
100g of sugar
200g of frozen red fruits.
14 macaroons

Preparation

Preparation:
- Separate the whites from the yolks.
- Beat the yolks with the sugar until they are white.
- Add the mascarpone and beat the preparation to make it lighter.
- Beat the egg whites until stiff.
- Gently mix the snow with the preparation.
The verrines:
- Place 3 macaroon halves in the bottom of the glasses. Crush them slightly.
- On top, place the red fruits still frozen.
- Pour the preparation over the red fruits.
- Place in the refrigerator until the next day.
- Present the verrines accompanied by 2 macaroons that you will have garnished with a fruit filling (blackberry jelly + powdered sugar for example) and for the greediest, a raspberry coulis type sauce.

Tiramisu Banana Speculoos
verrines: 6

Preparation time: 20 min

Ingredients

250g of mascarpone
3 fresh eggs
200g of sugar
1 sachet of vanilla sugar
3 bananas
Spéculoos
g of coconut

Preparation

Put the 3 egg yolks in a bowl. Beat the eggs and add the mascarpone, then add the vanilla sugar and the sugar a little at a time, tasting so that the mixture is sweet enough for your taste.
Add the variant if desired.
Put the 3 egg whites in the bowl and beat them until stiff.
Gently fold the egg whites into the mascarpone mixture.
In a plate, mash the bananas and add sugar if necessary.
Put the banana mixture in the bottom of each glass and put the mascarpone on top.
Chill until ready to serve.
Just before serving, crush a few speculoos in a bowl and sprinkle the top of each verrine with it.

strawberry and palet bretons verrines
Serves 8

Preparation time: 30 min

Ingredients

250g of mascarpone
400g of strawberries
3 eggs
150g of Breton palets
1/2 lemon
50g brown sugar
30g powdered sugar
125g vanilla sugar

Preparation

Wash and cut the strawberries in small pieces.
Put them in a bowl with the lemon juice and powdered sugar, mix well and keep in a cool place.
Take the eggs and separate the whites from the yolks.
With the yolks, add the brown sugar and the vanilla sugar. Make the mixture
white and incorporate the mascarpone. Set aside.
Beat the egg whites until stiff and fold into the mascarpone mixture gently.
Coarsely crush the palets bretons.
Take pretty verrines and fill them with alternating layers of cakes, strawberries
and mascarpone mixtures.
Place in the refrigerator for 30 minutes.
To be enjoyed chilled.

Peach, cream and speculoos cup
Serves 6

Preparation time: 20 min

Ingredients

250g of mascarpone
500g cottage cheese
1 large can of peaches in syrup
200g of speculoos
100g brown sugar
1 packet of vanilla sugar

Preparation

First crush some speculoos and put them in the bottom of the ice cream cups.
In a bowl, mix the mascarpone with the cottage cheese, add the brown
sugar and the vanilla sugar and mix everything together.
Crush the speculoos and add the rest of the cottage cheese and 50g
of brown sugar, you will obtain a kind of paste.
Drain your peaches in syrup and rinse them with water, in a plate

cut them in pieces (not too big, not too small).
Then, start by placing the peach pieces in ice cream cups on top of the crushed speculoos.
On top of the peaches, add the speculoos paste (speculoos and cottage
cheese) and then put a layer of the mascarpone cream.
Since the pastry is difficult to spread with a pastry blender, I personally spread it with my fingers.
Decorate with peach pieces on top and speculoos crumbs.
Leave in the fridge for 4 or 5 hours, this is a dessert that should be
eaten the same day otherwise the fruit will soften.

Tiramisu with sponge cake and speculoos
Serves 6

Preparation time: 20 min

Ingredients

250g of mascarpone
80g of sugar
1 sachet of vanilla sugar
3 eggs
100g of speculoos
200g of sponge cake
20cl of strong cold coffee
1 tablespoon of whisky

Preparation

Separate the egg whites from the yolks.
Whisk the yolks with the sugars until the mixture whitens and then add the mascarpone.
In a separate bowl, whisk the egg whites until stiff, then fold
into the sugar mixture...but gently! Set aside.
In a dish, mix the coffee and whisky, dip the cookies in it as you go along, but very
quickly so as not to soak them too much, then arrange them in a rectangular dish.
Line the dish with a layer of sponge fingers, then a layer of cream, then another
layer of sponge fingers and speculoos, then the cream.
Place the tiramisu in the refrigerator for at least 4 hours. The longer it sits, the
better it is! Just before serving, crush some speculoos on top and enjoy!

Tiramisu of the Squirrel (hazelnuts and cookies)
Serves 6

Preparation time: 20 min

Ingredients

250g of mascarpone
80g of powdered sugar
2 eggs
1 sachet of vanilla sugar

20cl of milk
2 packages of hazelnut moon cookies
2 tablespoons hazelnut paste
tablespoon of praline

Preparation

Separate the whites from the yolks.
Whisk the yolks with the sugar until the mixture turns white.
Add the mascarpone and hazelnut paste and mix well.
Beat the egg whites with the vanilla sugar and, if necessary, a pinch of salt.
Gently fold into the previous mixture.
For the assembly, in order to obtain a tiramisu which does not fall apart, I line
a cake tin with cling film and I make the assembly upside down.
I lay out the mascarpone cream first, then the cookies, which have been
soaked in milk for 1 second. I finish with a layer of cookies.
After 4 hours in the refrigerator, turn out onto a cake plate, remove
the cling film and sprinkle with praline.

Tiramisu with speculoos, pear and almonds
Serves 6

Preparation time: 20 min

Ingredients

250g of mascarpone (1 jar)
3 eggs
50g of brown sugar
drop of vanilla extract (natural or flavored, as desired)
50g of almonds
4 pears
20 peculiar cookies (two packages to make sure you don't run out; quantity
to be adapted according to your taste)

Preparation

Prepare the day before.
In a plate, crumble a package of speculoos and sprinkle the cookies with water and two
tablespoons of vanilla extract. Let soak, adding more water or vanilla if necessary.
Peel the pears and cut them into small cubes.
Blend about 10 speculoos very finely and mix the powder with the pear pieces.
Separate the whites from the yolks.
In a bowl, whisk the egg yolks with the sugar and add the mascarpone. Mix
until smooth, then add the almond powder and mix again.
Beat the egg whites until stiff (with a pinch of salt).
Gently fold the egg whites into the mascarpone cream, taking care not to break them.
Line the bottom of a dish with vanilla speculoos, cover with mascarpone

cream, add a layer of pear, and add another layer of mascarpone cream. Finish
by sprinkling a few pieces of pear for decoration.
Set aside in a cool place for 10 hours.

Tiramisu raspberry white chocolate speculoos
Serves 6

Preparation time: 15 min

Ingredients

250g of Galbani mascarpone
3 eggs
25g of sugar
1 sachet of vanilla sugar
200g white chocolate
200g raspberries
250g of speculoos

Preparation

Melt the white chocolate in the microwave oven.
Break the eggs and separate the whites from the yolks. Whisk the egg yolks with the
sugar and vanilla sugar until the mixture whitens and doubles in volume.
Add mascarpone and melted white chocolate.
Whisk again.
Whisk the egg whites with a pinch of salt.
Fold the eggs into the previous mixture in two batches.
Coarsely crush the speculoos into pieces and place them in the bottom of the verrines.
Add a layer of cream.
Add a few whole raspberries.
Finish with a new layer of mascarpone cream to the top of the container.
Sprinkle with crushed Speculoos and place a raspberry in the center for decoration.
Place in the refrigerator for a minimum of 3 hours, or overnight at best.

Christmas cakes (Finland)
Serves 4

Preparation time: 20 min

Ingredients

250g molasses
250g butter (or margarine)
20g of white sugar
1 tablespoon ground cloves
1 tablespoon of ground coriander
1kg of flour

4 eggs
1 teaspoon of bicarbonate

Preparation

Boil the molasses with the spices, then let it cool.
Mix the eggs, sugar and butter. Mix everything together.
Let stand at least one night.
Roll out with a rolling pin and cut out with a cookie cutter.
Bake in medium oven for about 10 minutes.
Be careful not to burn them! If necessary, cover them with parchment paper.

Walnut cakes
cupcakes: 30

Preparation time: 20 min

Ingredients

250g of cracked nuts
4 eggs
30g of flour
30g cornstarch
100g of butter
250g sugar
1 tablespoon vanilla liquid
2 tablespoons of walnut or walnut liquor

Preparation

Mix one whole egg with 3 yolks (keep the whites) with the sugar and
melted butter, flour, cornstarch, Sarlanoix, vanilla and nuts.
Beat the egg whites until stiff and fold them gently into the mixture.
Fill the caissettes or molds to 3/4. You can add a walnut kernel to decorate.
Space them on the plate.
Bake in the oven at 210° C (gas mark 7) for 10 to 15 minutes (to be watched).

Speculoos pudding
Serves 8

Preparation time: 30 min

Ingredients

250g of breadrassis
60cl of milk
3 eggs
2 packets of vanilla sugar
25g of powdered sugar

1 apple
1 tablespoon of rum
100g of speculoos paste

Preparation

Preheat your oven to 180°C (thermostat 6).
Cut the stale bread into 3 to 4 cm cubes.
Mix the eggs, sugar, vanilla sugar, rum and milk.
Pour this mixture over the bread and leave to soak for about 30 minutes, stirring
regularly to help the bread soak.
Add the diced apple.
Generously butter a cake pan.
Pour half of the mixture into the bottom of the pan.
Spread the speculoos mixture on top (you can soften it for 15 seconds
in the microwave to make it easier to spread).
Pour the other half of the preparation and flatten the surface well with a spoon.
Bake for 45 minutes at 180°C (gas mark 6).

Pistachio cookies
cookies about: 20

Preparation time: 10 min

Ingredients

250g of shelled pistachios
200g sugar
2 egg whites
2 small spoons of honey
1 grated lemon peel

Preparation

Crush the pistachios finely, and mix them with the sugar, the grated lemon peel and the honey.
Separate the yolks from the egg whites.
Fold the unworked egg whites into the mixture, they should act as a
glue that amalgamates the pistachio-sugar mixture.
Save the yolk for a clever use in a recipe found on this site!
Use the dough to make balls and place them on a baking sheet lined with parchment paper.
Make them big enough and spaced out, as they spread out to form cookie-like shapes.
Bake at 180-200°C for 10-15 min, watching carefully.
Remove from the oven, let cool and harden for 5 min, and put them in an airtight box.

Delicious Christmas cake
Serves 8

Preparation time: 15 min

Ingredients

250g of grated potato or carrot
125g chopped hazelnuts
125g of flour
1 teaspoon of cinnamon
100g raisins
150g brown sugar
2 eggs
12.5cl of oil
100g of fresh cream (optional)
1 teaspoon of yeast

Preparation

Grate the potatoes, chop the hazelnuts.
Mix flour, yeast, cinnamon, raisins and sugar.
Preheat the oven to 180°C (gas mark 6), and butter a 24cm square mold.
Beat the eggs into a foam, then add the oil, potatoes and hazelnuts; and then the flour.
Bake for 40 minutes. Let cool and cover with fresh cream.
It's ready!

Macaroons

macaroons: 20

Preparation time: 20 min

Ingredients

250g almond powder
200g of sugar
1 tablespoon of honey
2 egg whites + 1 yolk
1 tablespoon of apricot or apple jelly
drop of vanilla liquid
1 teaspoon of bitter almond extract

Preparation

Mix the almonds, sugar, honey and vanilla in a mortar. Mix in the egg whites
little by little. The mixture should be of the same consistency as the almond
paste, so it may not be necessary to use all the egg whites.
Stir in the apricot jelly and bitter almond extract to finish and
let rest for 6 to 8 hours in the refrigerator.
Roll into a long roll 4 cm in diameter, cut into 2 cm thick slices and place on a baking
sheet covered with buttered parchment paper. Brown with egg yolk.
Cook at moderate heat (Th 6 or 180°C) for 20 mn, the small cakes must be of a golden blond.
Let cool completely.
Wrap each macaroon separately in a square of aluminum foil to keep it soft and fresh.

Provencal Macaroons
macaroons: 30

Preparation time: 20 min

Ingredients

250g almond powder
220g of powdered sugar
100g of boiled potato
Bitter almond extract (or another flavor, Grand Marnier, rum)
Candied cherries (or whole almonds)
1egg

Preparation

Put the almond powder and powdered sugar in a bowl, along with the chosen flavor.
Add the potatoes, previously crushed with a fork, and mix well to obtain a soft
dough (if the almond powder is a bit dry, add a knob of butter).
With the dough obtained, make walnut-sized balls and place them on a baking
sheet covered with parchment paper.
You can put half a candied cherry or an almond on the ball.
With a brush, pass beaten egg on the balls and put in the oven
(200°C - th 6 or 7) during 20 min; watch well!

Small cakes with ricotta and raspberries
Serves 12

Preparation time: 15 min

Ingredients

250g of ricotta
3 eggs
180g of sugar
75g of flour
75g almond powder
125g raspberries

Preparation

Preheat the oven to 180°C (thermostat 6).
Separate the egg whites from the yolks.
Beat the yolks with the sugar and then add the ricotta. Beat vigorously to remove lumps.
Add flour and almond powder.
Beat the egg whites until stiff and fold them gently into the mixture.
Butter or oil your muffin tins and fill them 2/3 full. Place 3 raspberries in each and press lightly.
Bake for 30 minutes. Let cool on a rack.

Cheesecake with fresh cream and speculos
Serves 8

Preparation time: 30 min

Ingredients

250g of speculoos
120g of semi-salted butter

Preparation

For the dough:
Crush the speculoos, add the melted butter, mix everything together and fill a mould (just the bottom, preferably removable, for unmoulding) with the dough thus obtained. Set aside.
For the preparation:
Place the two gelatin sheets in a bowl of cold water to soften. Set aside.
Mix the four yogurts and the fresh cream in a bowl.
Add 130 g of sugar and the vanilla sugar.
Clarify one egg. Whisk the egg white with a pinch of salt until you get a firm mousse.
Heat 30 g of sugar with a little water over very low heat until you obtain a sugar syrup.
Gently fold the syrup into the egg whites (while continuing to beat),
and fold into the rest of the mixture in two batches.
Mix the yolk with the cornstarch, the two sheets of softened gelatin, and lemon juice.
Heat, stirring well to obtain a smooth orange mixture. Stir into remaining mixture.
Fill the speculo pastry with the preparation.
Heat to 160°C (gas mark 5) in the oven for 35 to 40 minutes.
Take out and let rest in the fridge for 2 hours.
Bon appétit!

Pineapple speculoos mascarpone cheesecake
Serves 8

Preparation time: 30 min

Ingredients

250g of speculoos
125g of butter
500g of mascarpone
1/2 glass of caster sugar (100 g)
330g canned pineapple
3 sheets of gelatin
3 tablespoons fresh cream
teaspoon of lemon juice
teaspoon of lemon

Preparation

Crush the speculoos and mix them with the melted butter. Line the bottom of a springform pan (about 26 cm in diameter) with the mixture. Keep in a cool place.
Mix the mascarpone with the sugar and possibly the lemon zest and juice.
Drain the pineapples but keep the juice. Blend the pineapple to
a purée and add to the mascarpone mixture.
Put the gelatine leaves in cold water.
Heat 4 tablespoons of the pineapple juice. When the juice comes to a boil, dilute the gelatin sheets.
Then add to the mascarpone mixture.
Whip the cream until it is whipped. Gently add it to the mixture.
Pour this preparation on the speculoos base and keep in a cool place for at least
8 hours. The ideal is to make it the night before for the next day.

Tiramisu with speculoos and coconut
Serves 6

Preparation time: 30 min

Ingredients

250g of speculoos
250g of mascarpone
3 eggs
60g of powdered sugar
40cl of coconut milk
125g of grated coconut

Preparation

Separate the egg whites from the yolks in two dishes.
Mix the mascarpone with the egg yolks, the grated coconut and 100 ml of coconut milk.
Set aside.
Beat the egg whites until they are slightly soft.
Bring 4 tablespoons of water and the powdered sugar to a boil in a small saucepan.
As soon as the syrup boils, count 3 minutes of boiling, not more.
Remove from heat immediately and pour the boiling syrup over the egg
whites, whisking them continuously with an electric mixer.
Continue the process until the egg whites have cooled.
Gently fold the egg whites into the mascarpone and coconut cream.
Spread half of the speculoos in the bottom of a baking dish.
Sprinkle with 150 ml of coconut milk.
Cover with half of the mascarpone and coconut cream.
Top with the other half of the speculoos, drizzle with the remaining 150 ml of coconut
milk and finish with the other half of the mascarpone-coconut cream.
Place in the refrigerator for at least 4 hours.

Ricotta and speculoos cheesecake
Serves 8

Preparation time: 30 min

Ingredients

250g of speculoos
3 eggs, white and yellow separated
115g melted butter
500g ricotta cheese
100g heavy cream
125g sugar
1 teaspoon vanilla extract

Preparation

Preheat the oven to 180°C.
Crush the speculoos until they are not too big. Mix them with the melted butter and spread
this mixture on the bottom of a mould, making it rise a little on the edges. Refrigerate.
Mix the ricotta, cream, egg yolks, vanilla extract and sugar in a bowl.
Fold in the beaten egg whites.
Pour the mixture into the baking pan on top of the cookies.
Bake for about 1 hour.
It is normal that the cake is not completely set in the middle.
Let cool in the turned off oven (one hour) then take it out and let it cool completely.
Refrigerate for 12 hours.

Pineapple Financiers
Serves 6

Preparation time: 10 min

Ingredients

250g sugar
100g of flour
100g almond powder
1 sachet of vanilla sugar
2 pinches of baking powder
8 egg whites
130g butter
150g pineapple pieces

Preparation

In a large container mix all the flour, sugar (icing or normal), almond powder and vanilla sugar.
Add the 8 egg whites and stir to mix well.
Cook the butter until it has a nice hazelnut color.
Let it cool down a little, then add it to the previous mixture.
Let the dough rest for at least half an hour, during which time preheat
your oven to 180°C (thermostat 6).

When you pour the dough into the moulds, add the pineapple.
The cooking will take between 20 and 30 minutes.

Financiers (gluten free and butter free)

pieces: 15

Preparation time: 40 min

Ingredients

250g sugar
110g almond powder
140g of coconut oil
100g of coconut flour
8 egg whites
Salt

Preparation

Mix the sugar, coconut flour and almond powder.
Melt the coconut oil and add it to the mixture.
Beat the egg whites with a good pinch of salt.
Mix the whites and the batter very gently, otherwise the financiers
will be more doughy and less airy.
Butter metal molds or financial molds, and pour the batter into them.
Bake for 18 minutes.

Bear paws (cookie)

cookies: 50

Preparation time: 15 min

Ingredients

250g sugar
125g of grated chocolate
2 eggs
250g almond powder
1 teaspoon of cinnamon (10 g)

Preparation

Blanch the eggs and the sugar.
Add almonds and cinnamon and mix with a fork.
Add the grated chocolate.
Put the dough in a cool place in aluminum foil for 1 night.
Using your fingers, form small piles and place them on parchment paper.
Bake for 15 minutes at 180°C (gas mark 6).

Melt-in-the-mouth terrine with pink Reims cookies
people: 8

Preparation time: 10 min

Ingredients

250g of caster sugar
300g of almond powder
250g of pink Reims cookie
5 eggs
300g of butter
cl of marc de Champagne

Preparation

Powder the pink cookies.
In a bowl, mix the sugar, the almond powder, the pink cookies powder. Add the whole
eggs, mix well, add the marc de Champagne (optional), then add the butter.
Mix well...
Prepare a cake mold lined (lined) with cling film, pour the preparation in
it, put a cling film on it, keep in a cool place for 24 hours...
Cut into slices and serve with vanilla flavored custard or Champagne marc...
Bon appétit!

Terrine chocolate speculoos without oven
people: 6

Preparation time: 15 min

Ingredients

25 speculoos cookies
200g dark chocolate
100g of salted butter
100g powdered sugar
4 egg yolks
Bitter cocoa

Preparation

Melt the chocolate with the butter in a saucepan.
In a bowl, whisk the egg yolks, sugar and a tablespoon of cocoa.
Add the chocolate/butter mixture, gradually and while mixing.
Finally, add 20 coarsely crumbled speculoos.
Pour the mixture into a cake tin, cover and leave in the fridge for 12 hours.
Then turn out.
Crumble the remaining 5 speculoos and cover the terrine with them.
Finally, sprinkle with cocoa powder to even out the surface.

It's ready!

Orange Oatmeal Muffins

pieces approx.: 12

Preparation time: 25 min

Ingredients

25cl oatmeal
12.5cl orange juice (fresh if possible)
12.5cl boiling water
orange zest
12.5cl melted butter
12.5cl brown sugar
12.5cl sugar
2 eggs
25cl of raisins
30cl of flour
1 sachet of yeast
1 teaspoon of bicarbonate (optional)
1 teaspoon of salt
1 teaspoon vanilla extract
Rum

Preparation

Soak the grapes in the rum (at least 1/2 day).
Soak the oats in the orange juice and boiling water for 15 minutes.
Add the orange zest.
Beat the eggs into the oatmeal mixture and stir in the drained raisins (save the rum).
In a bowl, combine flour, baking powder, baking soda, brown sugar, sugar, salt and melted butter.
Add vanilla and 2 tablespoons of the rum used to macerate the raisins.
Bake for 20 to 25 minutes at 190°C (gas mark 6-7) or until golden brown on top.

Raspberry muffins with soy milk

Serves: 4

Preparation time: 15 min

Ingredients

25cl vanilla soymilk
250g sifted wholemeal flour
1 egg
6cl of oil
1/2 teaspoon of yeast
2 tablespoons raisins
1 teaspoon of lemon grated

150g of raspberries
Butter for the mussels

Preparation

Preheat the oven to thermostat 6 (180°C).
In a bowl, put the flour mixed with the yeast.
Pour the egg in the center, the vanilla soy milk and the oil.
Gradually add to the flour.
Add the raisins, lemon zest and finally the raspberries.
Mix everything together and pour into lightly buttered muffin tins or ramekins.
Bake in a medium oven for 20 minutes, checking with the tip of a knife.

Chocolate-covered almond tuiles

Serves 6

Preparation time: 15 min

Ingredients

25g butter
100g sugar
80g of flour
2 packets of vanilla sugar
3 egg whites
75g of flaked almonds

Preparation

Preheat the oven to 165°C (thermostat 5-6).
In a bowl, mix the butter and sugars. Add the egg whites. Add the flour and almonds.
Cover a baking sheet with baking paper and make small piles of dough spaced far
apart from each other and flatten the piles with the back of a spoon.
Bake for 10 minutes.
Take the tiles out of the oven and put them on a rolling pin to give them the rounded shape of tiles.
Melt the chocolate with a little water, add the powdered sugar off the heat. Mix well.
Dip the end of the tiles in the chocolate and let cool.

Chocolate and bergamot cookie rolls

Serves 6

Preparation time: 1h30

Ingredients

25g of cocoa powder
4 eggs
100g sugar
50g of flour

15g of butter

Preparation

Preheat the oven to 210°C (thermostat 7).
Whisk the egg yolks with the sugar, then the cocoa and the flour, then the egg whites.
Spread the dough on a sheet of parchment paper and bake for
10 minutes in the middle of the oven.
Turn the cookie over on a wet cloth and roll.
Melt the chocolate. Bring 10 cl of cream to the boil, pour in the tea, leave to infuse
covered for 5 min and filter.
Soften gelatine and put it in the chocolate. Add the hot cream.
Whip the rest of the cream into a firm whipped cream and add it to the cooled preparation.
Unroll the cookie, remove the paper, spread 3/4 of the mousse, roll
up, wrap in cellophane film and chill for 1 hour.
After one hour, cover with the rest of the mousse. Serve or keep chilled until serving time.

Vanilla fruit gazpacho with orange tiles
Serves: 4

Preparation time: 30 min

Ingredients

25g white powdered sugar
25g brown sugar
25g of butter
25cl orange juice
25g of flour

Preparation

Melt the butter and keep it warm. Put the white sugar and brown sugar
in a bowl and add the hot butter. Mix it all together.
Add the orange juice and the sifted flour, mixing well so that
no lumps form. Set aside in a cool place.
Put the olive oil in a bowl. Place the vanilla bean in a plate and gently scrape out the
small vanilla seeds along the bean with a knife. Add them to the oil. Set aside.
Place strawberries, raspberries, bell pepper, tomato, ice and powdered sugar
in a blender. Blend until the mixture is smooth and airy.
Set aside in a cool place.
Heat oven to 180°C (gas mark 6).
Take the first preparation. Using a large spoon, spread the equivalent of a large
teaspoon of the mixture on a baking sheet in the shape of a tile.
Do this 4 times to obtain one tile for each person. Place in hot oven for
4-5 minutes maximum. Remove the tiles and set aside.
Put the gazpacho in 4 bowls, add 5 raspberries in a circle in each bowl.
Put half a tablespoon of vanilla oil on the raspberries.

Place the tile on the edge of the bowl in balance.

Blackberry and pineapple muffins
muffins about: 20

Preparation time: 30 min

Ingredients

260g flour
180g sugar
150g blackberries
125g of butter
2 eggs
2 teaspoons baking powder
2 teaspoons cinnamon powder
20cl of milk
1 teaspoon vanilla liquid

Preparation

For the muffins:
Pour the flour, baking powder and cinnamon into a bowl and mix.
Preheat the oven to 180°C (gas mark 6).
In a bowl, whisk the sugar with the softened butter until the mixture turns white.
Add the whole eggs and vanilla, then mix in the flour and yeast, gradually adding
the warmed milk.
Mix and add the blackberries.
Pour the batter into buttered high-sided molds and bake for 20 minutes.
For the pan:
Set up 2 pans. In one, caramelize the pineapple cut into small pieces over medium
heat for 10 minutes.
In another, melt the butter and add the blackberries. Cook, stirring gently, for 3 minutes.
Add the honey and stir in the pineapple, then leave on the heat for another 1 min.
Place one muffin on each plate with the hot pan.

Prune and Fibre Muffins (no butter or sugar!)
Serves 6

Preparation time: 10 min

Ingredients

260g flour
2 eggs
1 packet of baking powder
1 pinch of salt
15cl of water

Prunes (as much as you want)
Flax seeds
Muesli
Wheat bran (as much as you like! you can even put a little of everything!)

Preparation

Preheat the oven to 190°C (thermostat 6-7).
Put the flour, yeast, salt, prunes and flaxseed and/or muesli in a bowl.
In a second bowl, beat the eggs with the water.
Invert the second bowl into the first and stir until the flour is moistened
(it should not be too liquid but still be well mixed).
If necessary, add a little more water.
Fill muffin tins 3/4 of the way and place in the oven.
Wait 15 to 25 minutes until the muffins are cooked and then unmold to enjoy!

Almond Lemon Cupcakes
cupcakes: 23

Preparation time: 50 min

Ingredients

260g powdered sugar
240g of flour
80g of butter
25cl of milk
100g almond powder
2 eggs
1 tablespoon of yeast
1 pinch of salt
2 teaspoons of bitter almond extract

Preparation

Preheat your oven to 180°C.
In a bowl, mix the flour, sugar, yeast, almond powder, and pinch of salt with
the butter (with a mixer or by hand). You will obtain a sandy dough.
In a bowl, whisk the eggs into the milk. Add 3/4 of the milk/egg mixture to the batter and
mix with an electric mixer. Add the rest, and mix until you have a smooth dough.
Add the two teaspoons of bitter almond extract, and mix one last time.
Line your muffin tins with paper liners and fill them with batter (be careful
not to put too much in, or it will overflow into the oven!).
Bake for about 20 minutes, checking on the baking time from time to time.
Let cool completely before moving on to the icing.
Put your soft butter in a bowl, and whip it with an electric mixer. Add the confectioners'
sugar a little at a time while continuing to whip.
Squeeze a lemon and add the juice to the icing sugar/lemon mixture. Add a few drops of coloring
to give a nice yellow color, and fill a piping bag with the icing and decorate your cupcakes.

If you like, add a marzipan decoration, I chose to make a pink flower.
Your cupcakes are ready!

Alsatian Christmas cakes or schwowebredele

people: 6

Preparation time: 2 h

Ingredients

270g of butter
250g of sugar
2 eggs
1cinnamon
150g almond powder
500g of flour
candied orange peel
Aniseed

Preparation

Prepare the dough the day before:
Mix the flour, butter, almond powder, eggs, cinnamon and sugar in a bowl with your hands.
Put in the fridge during the night.
Preheat oven to 180°C (gas mark 6).
The next day, roll out the dough in small portions and cut out with small cookie cutters (heart, star...).
You can incorporate bits of candied orange peel or aniseed.
Brush with egg yolk.
Place in the oven on a rack for about 10 minutes.

Apricot and strawberry shortbread

Serves 6

Preparation time: 30 min

Ingredients

270g of butter + butter for the moulds
250g of powdered sugar
1 teaspoon of liquid vanilla extract
2 eggs
250g flour + flour for the molds
1/2 sachet of baking powder
2 tablespoons of milk
90g apricot jam
350g strawberries
2 tablespoons of powdered sugar

Preparation

Preheat the oven to 180°C (th. 6).
In a bowl, work the butter with the powdered sugar and the vanilla extract
until you obtain a creamy mixture. Incorporate the eggs one by one.
Sift together the flour and the yeast. Stir in the mixture without making
lumps, then dilute with the milk.
Butter and flour two 20 cm diameter moulds, spread the mixture in them and bake for 30
minutes. Leave to cool out of the oven, then remove from the moulds and leave to cool on a rack.
Prepare the vanilla whipped cream: whip the cream until stiff, gently folding
in the powdered sugar and vanilla extract as it begins to rise.
Gently flatten one of the shortbread biscuits into a flat surface. Heat the apricot jam
and brush it over the flattened cookie. Coat it with the vanilla whipped cream.
Reserve 8 beautiful strawberries. Cut the others into strips.
Arrange them on the whipped cream. Place the second shortbread on top, sprinkle
with powdered sugar and decorate with the reserved strawberries.

Cocoa and pistachio spiral cookies

Serves 6

Preparation time: 30 min

Ingredients

270g of flour
150g of sugar
100g of butter
1 egg
30g of cocoa
2 tablespoons of milk
2 teaspoons of natural vanilla flavouring

Preparation

Preparation of the cocoa paste.
Mix all the ingredients in a bowl and work the paste with your hands.
Preparation of the pistachio paste.
Mix all the ingredients in a bowl and work the paste with your hands.
Line the two doughs and keep them in a cool place (about 1 hour).
Flour the work surface and roll out the 2 pieces of dough to form 2 squares of about 2 mm thick.
Place the 2 squares of dough on top of each other.
Cut the resulting square in 2 and place the 2 halves on top of each other again.
Roll out thinly with a rolling pin and then roll the dough to form a sausage.
Wrap the dough in plastic wrap and keep in a cool place.
Preheat oven to 160°C (gas mark 5-6).
Cut the dough into slices of about 5 mm thick.
Place the slices on a baking sheet covered with baking paper and bake for 15 minutes.

Vanilla / chocolate swirl cookies
Cookies: 30

Preparation time: 40 min

Ingredients

270g flour
150g sugar
120g of butter
1 egg
3 tablespoons of milk
30g of cocoa

Preparation

Mix all the ingredients in a bowl and work the dough with your
hands until you obtain a ball of dough.
Shape the dough into a ball and chill for 30 minutes.
Mix all the ingredients in a bowl and work the dough with your
hands until you obtain a ball of dough.
Wrap the ball of dough in plastic wrap and chill for 30 minutes.
Preheat the oven to 160°C (gas mark 5-6) and make small balls of dough of each color.
Alternate 8 small balls of dough of different colors, forming circles. Glue the 8 balls
together and flatten between your hands, turning slightly to obtain a spiral effect.
Place on a baking sheet covered with baking paper.
Bake for 15 minutes.

Nutella Heart Muffins
muffins: 12

Preparation time: 10 min

Ingredients

280g of flour
1/2 sachet of baking powder
1 pinch of salt
2 eggs
100g of powdered sugar
1 sachet of vanilla sugar
100g melted butter
10cl of milk
1 plain yogurt
1 small jar of nutella (or other chocolate spread)
Butter and flour for the mould

Preparation

Preheat your oven to 180°C. In a bowl, mix the flour, baking powder and salt.
In another bowl, beat the eggs with a whisk, then add the powdered sugar and the vanilla sugar.
Pour the melted butter over the mixture, stirring constantly, then add the milk and yogurt.
Stir in the first flour-yeast-salt mixture.
Butter and flour the muffin tin, fill it 1/3 full with the mixture, form a small bowl,
place a nutella nut in the center and cover with the remaining batter.
Bake the muffins for about 20 minutes.
Take them out and wait 5 minutes before unmolding them. Can be eaten slightly warm.

Muffins of kings (frangipane)
pieces: 10

Preparation time: 15 min

Ingredients

280g of flour
1/2 sachet of baking powder
1 pinch of salt
2 eggs
100g of powdered sugar
100g melted butter
1 plain yogurt
10cl of milk
1 teaspoon of bitter almond extract

Preparation

Preparation: Frangipane
Take all the ingredients, mix them in a bowl, work and add ingredients according
to the desired texture: a thick paste but not too much either.
Muffins:
In a bowl, mix the flour, baking powder and salt. In another bowl, beat the eggs with the
sugar with a whisk. Pour in the melted butter, yogurt and milk. Mix well (insist on the
bottom). Add the mixture to the first bowl and mix until the dough is smooth.
Pour 2/3 of the batter into the pan. Then put the equivalent of a teaspoon in the
center of the batter, and cover. Then take a spoon, and go around each mold with it,
pressing against the edge (so that the two layers of dough adhere better)
Bake for 15 minutes at 180°c
Place a small bead or a small bean in the center of one of the muffins if it's galette day!

Klipferle (Small Alsatian shortbread horseshoes)
Serves 8

Preparation time: 15 min

Ingredients

280g of flour
100g almond powder
50g of powdered sugar
1 sachet of vanilla sugar
200g of butter

Preparation

Quickly mix the flour, almond powder, powdered sugar, vanilla sugar and butter with your fingers.
Form a ball and let it rest in the refrigerator for 1 hour in cling film.
Preheat oven to 180°C.
On a lightly floured surface, roll out the dough to a thickness of 5 mm. Cut out rectangles of about 1.5 cm x 8 cm. Lay them out flat, rounding them slightly to form small horseshoes.
Place them on a baking sheet covered with buttered parchment paper and bake them for 5 to 8 minutes maximum. They must not brown at all!
After they have cooled down completely, roll them in vanilla sugar and enjoy them with tea or coffee.
Sublissive!

Deer cookies
Serves 6

Preparation time: 15 min

Ingredients

280g of flour
100g of sugar
100g of half salt butter
2 eggs
1/2 sachet of baking powder
20 sweets

Preparation

Preheat the oven to 200° (thermostat 6-7)
Mix the flour, baking powder and sugar in a bowl.
Crush the deer into small pieces.
Add the butter, eggs and pieces of deer, then work with a fork.
Roll out the dough between two sheets of parchment paper
and cut out shapes with a cookie cutter.
Place them on a baking sheet on parchment paper.
Place in the oven for about 8 minutes (watch).

Deer Muffins
Muffins: 12

Preparation time: 10 min

Ingredients

280g of flour
100g of powdered sugar
100g melted butter
125g cottage cheese (0% or with fat)
10cl of milk
2 eggs
1 sachet of baking powder
1 sachet of vanilla sugar
12daim

Preparation

Sift the flour, baking powder and salt in a bowl.
In a separate bowl, beat the eggs, adding the powdered sugar and the vanilla sugar little by little.
Pour the melted butter into this mixture. Add the cottage cheese and milk.
Pour this mixture into the bowl containing the flour, baking powder and salt.
Let the mixture rest for 1 hour in the fridge covered with cling film.
Preheat your oven to 180°C (thermostat 6).
Butter and flour the muffin tins.
Fill your molds to 1/3, cut a chocolate deer in 4 pieces, put 2 pieces of deer in the molds lined with dough, then cover with the remaining dough. Finish with 2 pieces of deer on top of each muffin, pressing them in slightly.
Bake the muffins for about 20 minutes.
Remove from the oven and wait 5 minutes before removing from the pan and eating while still warm.

Cherry Muffins
Serves 6

Preparation time: 10 min

Ingredients

280g flour
150g brown sugar or powdered sugar
400g pitted cherries (cherries straight from the tree)
25cl of semi-skimmed milk
90g of butter
2 eggs
1 packet of baking powder
1 pinch of salt

Preparation

Mix the flour, brown sugar, baking powder and salt in a bowl.
In another bowl, mix the melted butter, milk and eggs. Pour this mixture

THE FRENCH COOKIE BAKEBOOK

into the first bowl. Mix until the mixture becomes smooth.
Add the pitted cherries and mix together. Pour into the muffin cups.
Bake for 20 minutes at 200°C (gas mark 6).

All chocolate muffins with white heart
muffins: 20

Preparation time: 15 min

Ingredients

280g of flour
2 eggs
100g butter
100g of powdered sugar
10cl of milk
1 sachet of vanilla sugar
1/2 sachet of baking powder
1 pinch of salt
3 teaspoons of bitter chocolate powder
1 bar of white chocolate

Preparation

Preheat the oven to 180°C (gas mark 6).
In a bowl, mix the flour, salt and yeast.
In another bowl, beat the eggs, add the sugar and the vanilla sugar.
Melt the butter, then add it to the second bowl while stirring. Add the milk and the first mixture.
Pour in the bitter chocolate.
Butter the moulds and fill them to 2/3. Place a square of white chocolate in the dishes.
Bake the muffins for 15 minutes at 180°C (gas mark 6).

Muffins heart spread with Thermomix
muffins: 12

Preparation time: 10 min

Ingredients

280g of flour
2 eggs
100g butter
100g of powdered sugar
1 plain yogurt
10cl of milk
1 sachet of vanilla sugar
12 teaspoons of chocolate spread
1/2 sachet of baking powder

1 pinch of salt

Preparation

Preheat your oven to 180 °C (th. 6).
Put the butter in the bowl of your Thermomix and melt it for 5 min / 60 °C / speed spoon.
Add the eggs and sugars, then beat for 15 sec / 0 °C / speed 7.
Add the flour, baking powder, yogurt, milk and pinch of salt and mix for 30 sec / 0 °C / speed 7.
Pour the batter 2 cm high into lightly greased muffin tins or baking trays. Place 1
teaspoon of batter in the center of each muffin, then pour back 1 to 2 cm of batter.
Do not fill the pans completely, as the cakes will puff up during baking.
Bake for 20 minutes and serve after cooling.

Cookeo heart muffins
muffins: 12

Preparation time: 10 min

Ingredients

280g of flour
2 eggs
100g butter
100g of powdered sugar
1 plain yogurt
10cl of milk
1 sachet of vanilla sugar
12 teaspoons of chocolate spread
1/2 sachet of baking powder
1 pinch of salt

Preparation

Preheat your oven to 180°C (th. 6).
Put the butter in the bowl of your Companion and melt it.
Add the eggs and the sugars, then beat.
Add the flour, baking powder, yogurt, milk and pinch of salt while mixing.
Pour the batter 2 cm high into lightly buttered muffin tins or baking trays. Place 1
teaspoon of batter in the center of each muffin, then pour back 1 to 2 cm of batter.
Do not fill the molds completely, as the cakes will puff up during baking.
Bake for 20 minutes and serve after cooling.

Mister Cuisine heart muffins
muffins: 12

Preparation time: 10 min

Ingredients

280g flour
2 eggs
100g butter
100g of powdered sugar
1 plain yogurt
10cl of milk
1 sachet of vanilla sugar
12 teaspoons of chocolate spread
1/2 sachet of baking powder
1 pinch of salt

Preparation

Preheat your oven to 180 °C (th. 6).
Put the butter in the bowl of your Monsieur Cuisine and melt it for 5 min / speed 1 / 60°C.
Add the eggs and sugars, then beat for 15 sec / speed 7 / 0 °C.
Add the flour, baking powder, yoghurt, milk and a pinch of salt and mix for 30 sec / speed 7 / 0 °C.
Pour the batter 2 cm high into lightly buttered muffin tins or baking trays. Place 1
teaspoon of batter in the center of each muffin, then pour back 1 to 2 cm of batter.
Do not fill the molds completely, as the cakes will puff up during baking.
Bake for 20 minutes and serve after cooling.

Companion Heart Spread Muffins
muffins: 12

Preparation time: 10 min

Ingredients

280g flour
2 eggs
100g butter
100g of powdered sugar
1 plain yogurt
10cl of milk
1 sachet of vanilla sugar
12 teaspoons of chocolate spread
1/2 sachet of baking powder
1 pinch of salt

Preparation

Preheat your oven to 180 °C (th. 6).
Put the butter in the bowl of your Companion and melt it with the mixer / speed 3 / 60 °C / 5 min.
Add the eggs and sugars, then beat with the ultrablade / speed 7 / 0 °C / 15 sec.
Add the flour, baking powder, yoghurt, milk and a pinch of salt while mixing
with the ultrablade / speed 7 / 0 °C / 30 sec.
Pour the batter 2 cm high into lightly buttered muffin tins or baking trays. Place 1

teaspoon of batter in the center of each muffin, then pour back 1 to 2 cm of batter.
Do not fill the molds completely, as the cakes will puff up during baking.
Bake for 20 minutes and serve after cooling.

Cooking Chef Heart Spread Muffins
muffins: 12

Preparation time: 10 min

Ingredients

280g flour
2 eggs
100g butter
100g of powdered sugar
1 plain yogurt
10cl of milk
1 sachet of vanilla sugar
12 teaspoons of chocolate spread
1/2 sachet of baking powder
1 pinch of salt

Preparation

Preheat your oven to 180 °C (th. 6).
Put the butter in the bowl of your Cooking Chef and melt it with
the K mixer tool / 4 min / 60 °C / speed 2.
Add the eggs and sugars, then beat with the mixer tool K / 25 sec / 0 °C / speed 6.
Add the flour, baking powder, yoghurt, milk and a pinch of salt while mixing
with the mixer tool K / 50 sec / 0 °C / speed 6.
Pour the batter 2 cm high into lightly buttered muffin tins or baking trays. Place 1
teaspoon of batter in the center of each muffin, then pour back 1 to 2 cm of batter.
Do not fill the molds completely, as the cakes will puff up during baking.
Bake for 20 minutes and serve after cooling.

Very simple muffins
Serves 12

Preparation time: 15 min

Ingredients

280g of flour
2 eggs
100g of sugar
150ml of milk
80g of butter (or 8 tablespoons of oil)
1 sachet of baking powder

1 sachet of vanilla sugar
1 pinch of salt
Cinnamon
Vanilla extract
Brandy, etc...)

Preparation

In a first bowl: mix flour, sugar, salt, vanilla sugar and yeast.
In a second bowl: mix the milk, oil (or melted butter) and eggs.
Pour the contents of the second bowl into the first and stir until you
have a fairly smooth batter. Leave some small lumps.
Put in the oven for 15 min at 180°C (thermostat 6).

Thick and chewy American cookies
small cookies: 20

Preparation time: 45 min

Ingredients

280g of flour
5g baking powder (1 teaspoon)
7.5g of cornstarch
1 pinch of salt
170g of butter
100g of blond or brown vergeoise (important for the softness)
70g powdered sugar
1 egg yolk + 1 yolk
10g vanilla extract (2 teaspoons)
Chocolate at will (I use 100g)
Peanut
Almonds
Nuts
Dried fruits...

Preparation

Melt the butter, mix it with the sugars (vergeoise+normal), then add the egg, the
yolk, the salt and the liquid vanilla (taking care that the butter-sugar mixture is not
too hot so as not to cook the eggs). Mix everything together with a whisk.
On the other hand, mix the flour, yeast and cornstarch. Add this mixture to
the previous preparation and mix well. Then add the sprinkles.
Form small (or large) round balls (do not flatten) and place them on a baking sheet on
greaseproof paper and freeze for 30 minutes. Preheat your oven to 170°C (thermostat 6).
After 30 minutes take the tray out of the freezer and put it in the oven for 11
minutes. Remove the parchment paper from the baking sheet and put the cookies on
a plate as soon as you can pick them up without breaking them too much.

Ricotta mousse on a bed of macaroons
Serves 8

Preparation time: 30 min

Ingredients

280g of macaroons
50cl of fresh cream
250g of caster sugar
1 lime
2 yellow lemons
100g of ricotta cheese

Preparation

Crush the macaroons into small pieces.
Whip the cream until stiff.
In a bowl, mix the ricotta with the caster sugar, the zest of the lime and the juice of the lemons.
Gently fold in the whipped cream.
Make a bed with the macaroons in the bottom of ramekins and pour the preparation gently on top.
Cover with cling film and refrigerate for 12 hours.
Serve well chilled.

Banana cookies - Gluten free, sugar free and butter free
cookies: 30

Preparation time: 1h20

Ingredients

2 bananas
100g chestnut flour
120g of rice flour
20g white almond powder
8g of bicarbonate
100g oatmeal
1 pinch of salt
1 teaspoon of gluten free baking powder
2 eggs
1 teaspoon vanilla extract
150g of 70% chocolate
100g of odorless organic coconut butter

Preparation

Puree the bananas by mashing them with a fork.
Add the eggs and beat well until creamy.

Add 1 teaspoon of vanilla extract. Then add the coconut butter.
Mix well.
Sift the flours, almond powder, yeast and a pinch of salt.
Add to previous mixture.
Add chocolate chips to the mixture.
Place small pieces of dough on a baking sheet covered with parchment paper.
Bake at 180°C for 12 minutes (cookies are done when golden brown).
Enjoy them warm or store them in a box for a few days.

Banana, Apricot and Chocolate Muffins
Muffins: 12

Preparation time: 15 min

Ingredients

2 bananas
2 apricots
75g sugar
1 egg
1 sachet of yeast
150g of flour
75g melted butter
50g of grated chocolate
Cinnamon

Preparation

Preheat your oven to 190°C (thermostat 6/7).
Melt the butter in a saucepan over low heat.
Peel and cut the bananas into small pieces.
Wash, dry and dice the apricots.
In a bowl, mix the banana pieces and the diced apricots. Add the sugar
and the egg, lightly beaten, then the melted butter.
In a second bowl, mix the dry ingredients (flour, yeast, chocolate chips and cinnamon).
Gently fold the wet mixture into the dry mixture so that the
flour is no longer visible (mix very little).
Put the mixture in 12 buttered muffin cups and bake in a hot oven for 25 minutes.
Turn out and enjoy.

Verrine of cottage cheese, apple, banana and speculoos
Serves 3

Preparation time: 20 min

Ingredients

2 bananas

2 Canada apples
250g cottage cheese
5 speculoos
1 tablespoon sugar
1/2 vanilla bean
Lemon

Preparation

Peel the apples and cut them into pieces.
Heat a saucepan and throw in the apple pieces.
Add a tablespoon of water to prevent them from sticking.
Add the seeds of the vanilla bean and a little sugar and cover.
Do not over-stir to keep the apple pieces whole. Remove from
heat as soon as they are soft and caramelized.
Meanwhile, cut the banana into slices (not too thin).
Soak them in the lemon juice and then roast them in a pan. Add a little sugar.
Halfway through cooking, gently turn the banana slices over one by one without
crushing them. Remove from heat as soon as they are caramelized.
Crumble the 5 speculoos with your fingers and set aside.
Fill the verrines with a first layer of cottage cheese. Add a good layer of bananas. Spread a
layer of cottage cheese. Add a good layer of apples and finish with the crushed speculoos.
Leave in a cool place until serving.

Light banana and cookie verrine
Serves: 4

Preparation time: 15 min

Ingredients

2 bananas
300g of cottage cheese (0 or 20%, it's up to you...it's very good even with the 0%...)
4 tablespoons of sugar or sweetener
Cinnamon
12 butter with chocolate chips

Preparation

Prepare the cottage cheese with the sugar (or sweetener) and a good pinch of cinnamon.
Cut the bananas into slices.
Crush (in a freezer bag to avoid crumbs) the buttercups.
Prepare the verrines by alternating
- a layer of cottage cheese
- a layer of banana
- a layer of crushed cookies
Finish with a little grated chocolate.
Keep in a cool place.

Cookies oatmeal chocolate, coconut and banana

cookies: 10

Preparation time: 15 min

Ingredients

2 bananas
30g Gretel coconut cube
100g Gretel Organic Chocolate Porridge
30g of dark chocolate
2 tablespoons of soy milk

Preparation

Preheat the oven to 180°C (thermostat 6).
Peel the banana and cut it roughly.
Mix it with the crushed coconut cubes and the chocolate porridge. The dough
should be homogeneous and solid enough to be shaped into balls.
On a baking sheet covered with parchment paper, shape your cookies.
Then push a few pieces of your good dark chocolate into each cookie.
To give them a nice golden color, you can brush your cookies with the vegetable
milk of your choice before baking.
To give them a nice golden color, you can brush your cookies with the plant-
based milk of your choice before baking.There are less than 60 calories
per cookie, a good way to indulge without feeling guilty!

Banana and Pear Muffins

muffins: 12

Preparation time: 15 min

Ingredients

2 bananas
4pears
175g flour
1/2 sachet of yeast
100g brown sugar
60g of butter
2 eggs
10cl of milk
1 teaspoon of cinnamon (optional)
Liquid vanilla extract or 1 sachet of vanilla sugar

Preparation

Preheat your oven to 180°C (thermostat 6).
Slice the two bananas in a bowl and mix them with the two eggs, the melted butter and

the brown sugar. Mix vigorously with a fork, the bananas will crush themselves.
Add the flour and the yeast, mix well. Then add the milk. Finally add the vanilla,
cinnamon and chopped pears.
Put the dough in muffin tins.
Bake for about 20-25 min.
Let them cool on a plate and enjoy.

Banana cocoa muffins
muffins: 20

Preparation time: 15 min

Ingredients

2 ripe bananas
100g brown sugar
80g of soft butter
2 eggs
250g of flour
1 packet of baking powder
1 pinch of salt
2 tablespoons of cocoa
4cl of milk

Preparation

Mix (or mash) the bananas with 50 g of brown sugar, set aside.
Mix the butter and eggs with a mixer.
Add 50 g of brown sugar, mix and then pour the banana puree. Mix well.
In a bowl, mix flour with yeast and salt. Pour all at once into the first preparation and mix coarsely.
Separate the dough in two and add the cocoa to one of the bowls. If necessary
add 4 cl of milk to obtain an all chocolate dough.
Preheat the oven to 180 °C (gas mark 6).
Place the banana and cocoa batter in the muffin tins (fill 3/4 of the height of the tin).
Bake for about 15 minutes.
Let cool before unmolding and tasting.

cookies
cookies: 12

Preparation time: 15 min

Ingredients

2 egg whites
100g sugar
60g of flour
40g of butter

1 pinch of vanilla powder
1 pinch of salt

Preparation

- Whip the egg whites until stiff, with a pinch of salt.
- Carefully mix in the sugar, flour, melted butter and vanilla.
- Spoon the batter into small, spaced piles.
- Bake for 10 min in a hot oven at 200°, thermostat 6-7.

Almond Tuiles
Serves 4

Preparation time: 15 min

Ingredients

2 egg whites
100g powdered sugar
50g of flaked almonds
35g of butter
30g of flour

Preparation

Preheat your oven to 5/6.
Melt the butter and let it cool.
Beat the egg whites with the sugar without increasing.
Then add the flour and the melted butter (I use an electric mixer to save time).
On the baking sheet lined with buttered and floured baking paper, place small piles (the equivalent of a teaspoon) fairly far apart. Spread these small piles with the back of the spoon.
Sprinkle with slivered almonds.
Bake in the oven for 10 minutes at thermostat 5/6 (165°C). The tiles should be golden on the sides.
Remove the tiles and place them on a rolling pin to give them a domed shape.
A silicone baking sheet is ideal for this recipe.
To give the tiles the rounded shape, I roll the soft sheet directly onto the rolling pin and let it cool.
Just be careful when removing the tiles, as they break easily.

Meringues
Serves: 4

Preparation time: 30 min

Ingredients

2 egg whites
120g of powdered sugar
1 teaspoon of cornstarch
1 teaspoon of white wine vinegar

1 pinch of salt

Preparation

Preheat the oven to 150°C (thermostat 5).
Put the whites and salt in a bowl.
Whisk faster and faster.
When the mousse is very white and thick, add the sugar gradually and gently,
without stopping whisking until you get a very firm and shiny mousse.
Add the vinegar and the sifted cornstarch.
Immediately form piles on a non-stick baking sheet.
Bake for 1 hour. The meringues must be very light blond, dry above and below.
Let cool and then remove them from the baking paper.

Macaroons with almonds (petits fours)
Serves 6

Preparation time: 15 min

Ingredients

2 egg whites
125g of fine sugar
175g of ground almonds
1 teaspoon of cinnamon

Preparation

Beat the egg whites until stiff. Add sugar, almonds and cinnamon.
Using 2 spoons or a piping bag, place small piles on a baking sheet covered with parchment paper.
Bake in medium oven for about 10 minutes (watch).

Cinnamon macaroons
pieces: 12

Preparation time: 15 min

Ingredients

2 egg whites
125g powdered sugar
125g almond powder
1 teaspoon cinnamon powder
1 dash of lemon juice

Preparation

Sift the powdered sugar with the almond powder and the cinnamon.
Beat the egg whites until stiff. Gently fold in the sifted sugar and almond powder and lemon juice.
Use a pastry bag or spoon to form small, spaced piles on a parchment paper-lined baking sheet.
Let stand for at least 1 hour in a cool place.

Bake in the oven at 150°C (gas mark 5) for about 15 minutes.

Easy almond tuiles
tiles: 24

Preparation time: 20 min

Ingredients

2 egg whites
1 egg yolk
100g of sugar
1 sachet of vanilla sugar
50g of flour
80g melted butter
40g of flaked almonds

Preparation

Whip the egg whites until stiff with the sugars.
Gently fold in the flour and melted butter. Then the egg yolk and finally the almonds.
The dough obtained must be quite fluid.
Butter and flour a baking sheet. Place small piles of dough on top. Distribute the almonds evenly.
Bake for 5 minutes in a hot oven at 200° until the edges of the tiles are golden.
As soon as they come out of the oven, shape them on a rolling pin or a glass.

Quick cocoa meringues
pieces: 6

Preparation time: 10 min

Ingredients

2 egg whites
1 pinch of salt
125g powdered sugar
1 tablespoon of cocoa

Preparation

Take your eggs out preferably 1/4 hour before you start.
Beat your egg whites until stiff with the pinch of salt.
Slowly add the sugar while continuing to beat with an electric mixer.
Sprinkle the cocoa on top without stopping to whisk.
Arrange the meringues on a baking sheet with 2 tablespoons,
Bake at 120°C for 1 hour.

Amaretti (Italy)
Serves: 15

Preparation time: 20 min

Ingredients

2 egg whites
250g caster sugar
325g of blanched almonds
lemon zest
Margarine
2 tablespoons granulated sugar

Preparation

Heat the oven to 190°C.
Crush the almonds in a blender.
Lightly beat the egg whites with a fork. Mix them with the sugar
and add the almonds and the grated lemon peel.
Grease a baking sheet with margarine. Using a teaspoon, fill the baking
sheet with small discs, leaving enough space between them.
Sprinkle with granulated sugar and place in oven until golden brown (about 1/2 hour).
Store in an airtight (metal) box.

Egg white muffins
pieces: 4

Preparation time: 10 min

Ingredients

2 egg whites
40g flour
50g of sugar
1 sachet of vanilla sugar
Lemon + the complement in oil to reach 40 g

Preparation

Preheat the oven to 180°C (thermostat 6).
Mix the flour and the sugars.
Beat the egg whites until stiff. Add the whites to the sugar + flour mixture.
Add lemon juice and oil.
Mix well until the dough becomes soft and homogeneous. Pour the batter into muffin tins.
Bake for about 25 minutes. The muffins are cooked when they are lightly browned.

Violet and white chocolate macaroons
pieces approx.: 15

Preparation time: 30 min

Ingredients

2 egg whites
60g almond powder
110g powdered sugar
20g powdered sugar
Purple food coloring

Preparation

The day before, break the eggs and keep the whites in a cool place.
The next day, prepare the ganache: melt the white chocolate gently with the liquid cream in a bain-marie. Remove from the heat, pour in the violet aroma and set aside in a cool place.
Preheat the oven to 150°C (thermostat 5).
Then prepare the shells.
Pour the powdered almonds and powdered sugar into the blender and blend. Sift the almond powder and powdered sugar mixture directly onto the baking tray. Place the baking sheet in the oven for 5 to 7 minutes, then remove from the oven and let cool.
In a mixing bowl, whip the egg whites with an electric mixer. When the whites begin to stiffen, add the powdered sugar a little at a time while continuing to beat.
Then add the purple coloring. Smooth the mixture well. Sift the almond/ice sugar mixture over the beaten whites.
Mix the whole.
Fill the piping bag and place about 30 small balls on parchment paper on the baking sheet.
Leave the macaroons in a dry place for at least 1 hour to crust.
Put them in the oven for 10 to 12 minutes at 150°C (thermostat 5).
When you take them out of the oven, let a little water run between the paper and the baking sheet so that the shells come off.
Fill half of the shells with the ganache and assemble the macaroons. Keep them in a cool place for about 1 hour before eating them.

Dry meringues
Serves 6

Preparation time: 15 min

Ingredients

2 egg whites
60g powdered sugar
70g powdered sugar
2 packets of vanilla sugar
1 pinch of salt
Parchment paper

Preparation

Preheat the oven to 150°, thermostat 5.

Add the pinch of salt to the egg whites and beat them until stiff. When the foam is firm, add the vanilla sugar without stopping to whisk.
Stop whisking and add the powdered sugar and powdered sugar.
Mix everything with a spoon, being careful not to let the whites fall. The mixture must remain firm and homogeneous.
Line a baking sheet with parchment paper. Using two teaspoons, place small mounds of the mixture on top.
Put the meringues in the oven and immediately lower the temperature by 30°, thermostat 1.
The meringues should bake at 120°, gas mark 4, for 55 minutes.
When the meringues are done, turn off the oven, close the door and leave them inside for 1 hour.
(Do not close the oven door or they will soften.)

Orange Carrot Muffins

Serves: 6

Preparation time: 15 min

Ingredients

2 carrots
100g sugar
160g of flour
2 eggs
1 tablespoon of olive oil
10cl of light cream (15%)
1 packet of baking powder
2 teaspoons of natural orange flavor

Preparation

Peel, wash and grate the carrots.
Preheat the oven to 180°C (th6);
In a bowl, mix the sugar, flour and yeast.
Incorporate the eggs, oil, cream and aroma. Add the grated carrots.
Divide into 6 silicone muffin cups.
Bake for 20 minutes at 180°C (th6).

Cookies filled with hazelnut cream

Preparation time: 10 min

Ingredients

2 teaspoons of cocoa powder
2 tablespoons hazelnut puree
1 tablespoon of honey
1 large pinch of salt

Preparation

Prepare the hazelnut cream: In a bowl, mix the hazelnut puree, the cocoa, the honey and a pinch of salt until you obtain a homogeneous cream.
Heat a dry frying pan and toast the hazelnuts until the skins come off slightly. Pour the hazelnuts into the bowl of a blender and grind them into a powder.
Mix the flour, sugar, salt, 50g of hazelnut powder and one by one the tablespoons of water. You should obtain a dough that comes off well and does not stick too much.
Let rest 10 min in the fridge.
Lightly flour the work surface, then roll out the dough (neither too thin nor too thick) and cut out small circles with a small glass. Make an even number.
Place them on a baking sheet covered with baking paper and
bake at 180°C for 12 minutes, then let cool.
Spread a small spoonful of spread in the center, and close with another shortbread.
Do the same with the rest of the cookies.

Tiramisu with two cookies
Serves 4

Preparation time: 20 min

Ingredients

2 teaspoons sweetened cocoa
1 pinch of salt
2 eggs
125g of mascarpone
50g sugar
3cookiestout chocolate
3cookieschocolate hazelnuts
20cl of laitchocolate

Preparation

Separate the whites from the yolks.
Blanch the yolks with the sugar. Add the mascarpone and mix.
Beat the egg whites with a pinch of salt.
Gently add the egg whites to the mixture.
Mix gently until you obtain a homogeneous preparation.
In a bowl, break the cookies into small pieces.
For the dressing:
In 4 glasses, alternate 1 layer of cookies with 3 teaspoons of chocolate milk, 1 layer of cream, 1 layer of cookies with 3 teaspoons of chocolate milk, 1 layer of cream, 1 half teaspoon of unsweetened cocoa powder.
Let stand at least 4 hours in the refrigerator.

Low fat chocolate coffee cookies
cookies: 9

Preparation time: 20 min

Ingredients

2 tablespoons raw cocoa powder
1 tablespoon coffee
2 tablespoons hazelnuts
2 tablespoons cornstarch
100g brown sugar
1 cappuccino
1 egg
1/2 sachet of baking powder
3 boudoirs

Preparation

Preheat oven to 180°C (gas mark 6).
Break the egg and add the brown sugar. Whip well until you obtain a beige paste.
Add the cocoa, cornstarch, stick and yeast to the egg/sugar mixture. Mix well.
Crush the coffee and hazelnuts and add them to the mixture.
Break the boudoirs into large pieces and add to the mixture.
Mix everything together.
Spread small piles of the mixture on a baking sheet covered with parchment paper.
Bake for 20 to 30 minutes.
Wait for the cookies to cool completely before eating them.

Mug cake speculoos

Person: 1

Preparation time: 10 min

Ingredients

2 tablespoons flour
4 tablespoons speculoos
1 egg white
1 teaspoon of powdered sugar
1 teaspoon baking powder
5 tablespoons of milk
25g of semi-salted butter
Cinnamon or powdered sugar

Preparation

Melt the salted butter in a bowl (about 30 seconds)
Add the flour and baking powder to the butter bowl.
Mix (with a spoon, whisk or fork) well to get a homogeneous mixture.
In a separate bowl, crush the speculoos and add the milk to the bowl to create a sort of cream.
Add the speculoos/milk cream to the flour, baking powder and butter mixture.

Mix to remove any lumps.
In a separate bowl, beat the egg whites until stiff (we won't
use the yolks) + add the powdered sugar.
Fold the egg whites/icing sugar into the bowl.
Mix circularly (and gently for the fluffy side) so as not to break the egg whites.
Add cinnamon powder or vanilla sugar.
Mix for a homogeneous mixture.
Heat for 1m30/2 minutes in microwave.
Add broken speculoos for decoration.

Cocoa and 2 spice tuiles
small tiles: 20

Preparation time: 15 min

Ingredients

2 tablespoons wholemeal flour
2 tablespoons of sugar
2 tablespoons of low fat cream
1 teaspoon of armagnac
1 teaspoon unsweetened cocoa powder
Cinnamon to taste
grated nutmeg

Preparation

Mix everything together (if the dough is a little too compact, add a drop of milk).
Spread a sheet of baking paper on the baking sheet and place small piles of dough on it,
spaced out far enough so that they do not come together when they spread out.
Put in the oven at 180-200°C for 10 to 20 minutes (the tiles will be more
or less tender: be careful, they harden as they cool).

Raspberry, dark chocolate and coconut muffins
muffins: 12

Preparation time: 15 min

Ingredients

2 tablespoons cottage cheese
3 eggs
60g powdered sugar
50g melted butter
50g of grated coconut
1/2 sachet of baking powder
180g of flour
150g of dark chocolate

200g of fresh raspberries

Preparation

1) Preheat your oven to Th.7 (200°C).
In a bowl, mix the cottage cheese, eggs, sugar, melted butter, coconut, yeast and flour.
Chop the chocolate into chips. Add it to the mixture.
4) Gently fold in the raspberries.
Pour into muffin tins and bake for 15-20 minutes.

Pear and Speculoos Crispy Nems
Serves 4

Preparation time: 10 min

Ingredients

2 sheets of brick pastry
2 pears
60g ricotta cheese (or mascarpone)
20g of speculoos
40g brown sugar
50g of butter
Caramel

Preparation

Preheat the oven to 180°C (thermostat 6).
In a bowl, mix the ricotta, the pears cut into small pieces and the crumbled speculoos.
Place this mixture on the edge of the brick pastry sheets and roll up to form the egg rolls.
Brush with melted butter and sprinkle with brown sugar.
Bake for 20 minutes at 180°C.
Serve immediately topped with caramel!

Vanilla Madeleines without sugar
Serves 6

Preparation time: 20 min

Ingredients

2 vanilla beans
2 eggs
140g of soft butter + 15g for the molds (except if silicone)
100g of flour
1 pinch of salt

Preparation

Preheat the oven to 200°C (thermostat 6-7=).
Using a knife, cut the vanilla pods in half lengthwise.

Scrape the inside to remove all the seeds.
Separate the egg whites from the yolks and beat the whites until stiff.
Whip the butter to obtain a homogeneous mixture. Add the flour, egg yolks,
salt, vanilla seeds and finish by gently mixing with the egg whites.
Lightly grease the moulds and pour the batter halfway into the moulds. Don't put
too much dough, because the madeleines will swell up during baking.
Bake for 10 minutes. The madeleines should be golden and puffy. Let cool before unmolding.

Chocolate pear cupcakes

cupcakes: 40

Preparation time: 45 min

Ingredients

2 large cans of leek syrup
200g butter
250g sugar
6 eggs
350g of flour
1 sachet of yeast
100g of dark chocolate

Preparation

For the cake base :
Preheat the oven to 200°c. (thermostat 6-7)
Drain and dice the pears. Cut the chocolate into small pieces.
Mix the softened butter with the sugar, then whisk in the eggs one by one.
Add flour, baking powder, pears and chocolate.
Pour the preparation into cupcake molds (silicone or paper, be careful with
the quality of the paper because with the weight of the preparation, it can
overflow, otherwise double or even triple the thickness).
Bake at 200°c (thermostat 6-7) for about 30 min (adapt the baking time according to your oven).
For the glaze:
Cut the butter into small pieces. It should be soft enough to be worked more
easily with a whisk. Add the powdered sugar and milk. Whisk together.
Add a few drops of food coloring and continue whisking.
(I divide the icing into different bowls to vary the colors)
Remove the cupcakes from the oven and let them cool.
When cool, cover with frosting (you can add decorations) and refrigerate for 1 hour.

The helenettes

cookies: 4

Preparation time: 5 min

Ingredients

2 egg yolks
100g sugar
100g of flour
80g of butter
100g almond powder

Preparation

Preheat the oven to 200°C.
Melt the butter and let it cool. Work the egg yolks with the sugar.
Add the melted butter, flour and almonds.
Shape into balls and place on a baking sheet covered with parchment paper.
Bake in the oven for 8 to 10 minutes (watch for baking).

Small shortbread with cinnamon ultra easy
shortbread: 18

Preparation time: 15 min

Ingredients

2 egg yolks
1water
100g powdered sugar
150g of melted or softened butter
2cinnamon powder
10farina bombs
1 pinch of salt

Preparation

Preheat your oven to 200°.
In a bowl, mix the egg yolks, sugar, cinnamon and butter evenly with a whisk.
Add the spoonfuls of flour one by one, stirring well between each.
the dough should be thick and crumbly.
using a small spoon, place small piles of dough on an ovenproof baking sheet.
If your baking sheet is not non-stick, you can use parchment paper.
let cook 10 minutes approximately by plates
the shortbread are very fragile when they come out of the oven so you have to
remove them with a spatula and put them to cool down flat, or remove them
with the parchment paper and take them off once they are cold.
Can easily be stored for several days!

Ultra easy ginger shortbread
shortbread: 15

Preparation time: 15 min

Ingredients

2 egg yolks
1 water
100g powdered sugar
2 gingembreen powder
150g soft butter, softened or melted
10 farin
1 pinch of fine salt

Preparation

Preheat your oven to 200°.
In a bowl, mix the egg yolks, sugar, ginger and butter in a homogeneous way with a whisk.
Add the spoonfuls of flour one by one, stirring well between each.
the dough should be thick and crumbly.
using a small spoon, place small piles of dough on an ovenproof baking sheet.
If your baking sheet is not non-stick, you can use parchment paper.
let cook 10 minutes approximately by plates
the shortbread are very fragile when they come out of the oven so you have to
remove them with a spatula and put them to cool down flat, or remove them
with the parchment paper and take them off once they are cold.
Can easily be stored for several days!

Exotic Christmas shortbread

Serves 6

Preparation time: 30 min

Ingredients

2 egg yolks
250g of mascarpone
140g of butter
150g of flour
1 pinch of baking powder
25g of almonds
1 mango
1 raspberry pod
1 lime
140g powdered sugar
2 tablespoons of pistachios
1 teaspoon of cinnamon

Preparation

Beat the mascarpone with 60 g of powdered sugar and the lemon juice. Pour into silicone
moulds or directly onto a dish (cutting will be more difficult). Put in the freezer for 2 hours.
For the shortbread, mix the flour with the yeast, butter, almond powder, remaining
powdered sugar (80 g) and cinnamon. Mix in the egg yolks. Spread on a sheet

of baking paper for about 5 mm and refrigerate for 30 minutes.
Cut shortbread with a cookie cutter (or directly with a knife for artists) and bake for
12 minutes at thermostat 6 (180°C). Turn out the mascarpone pucks onto the cooled
shortbread. Add the diced mango, lime zest, a raspberry and pistachio slivers.

Seaweed shortbread with pistachio ice cream
Serves: 1

Preparation time: 35 min

Ingredients

2 egg yolks
50g of sugar
70g of semi-salted (or soft) butter
75g of flour
3g of baking powder
3g of nori
Sea milk)

Preparation

Prepare the shortbread:
Incorporate the ingredients in the order, mould it on 0,5 cm of thickness in a buttered mould.
Bake at 180°C for 10 minutes; turn out when lightly colored and let cool.
Prepare the sauce by mixing together the pistachios, honey, yogurt
and lemon until you have a liquid sauce.
It in a cool place until you are ready to serve the shortbread, drizzle with sauce just before eating.

Pistachio Breton biscuits
Shortbread: 15

Preparation time: 10 min

Ingredients

2 egg yolks
70g of sugar
80g of butter (semi-salted)
20g of honey
120g of flour
1/2 teaspoon of baking powder
150g of pistachios

Preparation

Preheat your oven to 180°C (th.6).
Beat the egg yolks with the sugar until the mixture whitens, then add the butter and the honey.
Sift the flour and the yeast and add them to the previous mixture with the pistachios.

Place the dough in muffin cases with a piping bag and smooth the surface roughly.
Bake in the oven for 15 minutes, then let cool and remove from the molds to cool.

Quick flutes
Cannelés: 10

Preparation time: 10 min

Ingredients

2 egg yolks + 1 whole egg
200g of sugar
1/2l of milk
Vanilla liquid or in pod
125g of flour
1 tablespoon of neutral oil
1 tablespoon of rum
Creamy butter for the mussels

Preparation

Blanch the eggs with the sugar and add the milk and vanilla.
Put in a saucepan and bring to a boil to obtain a 'crème anglaise'. Allow to cool.
Meanwhile, generously butter the molds and store in a cool place.
Preheat oven to 200°C.
Whisk the flour, oil and rum into the cooled mixture (which will have become
lumpy) until it is smooth.
Fill the moulds 3/4 of the way and bake for 45 to 55 minutes, depending
on the desired cooking time.

Cannelés inratables
cannelés: 60

Preparation time: 20 min

Ingredients

2l of milk
160g of butter
2 vanilla beans or vanilla powder
10 egg yolks
2 eggs
450g flour
50g cornstarch
800g powdered sugar
10cl of rum or another flavor
Powdered sugar for the moulds

Preparation

Prepare the dough the day before.
Beat the eggs in a large bowl and set aside.
Boil the milk with the butter and vanilla.
Immediately pour the milk over the beaten eggs while whisking. Let cool for a few hours.
Mix flour with cornstarch and powdered sugar.
Mix with the milk-egg mixture (hand whisk works very well) and add the rum.
Let the dough rest in the refrigerator for 24 hours.
After the dough is set, bake the cannelés.
Butter the molds (preferably copper) and line them with a thin layer of powdered sugar and tap to remove excess sugar.
Fill the molds to 1 cm from the edge.
Bake in the oven at thermostat 8 for 10 minutes and extend the baking time to about 50 minutes at thermostat 6.
Keep a close eye on the cooking to obtain the desired color.
Turn out hot and cool on a rack.

Meringue ice cream
Serves 6

Preparation time: 10 min

Ingredients

2meringues (medium)
100g sugar
4 eggs
50cl of liquid cream
40cl of caramelliquide

Preparation

- Put the whole eggs and the sugar in a bowl, mix until it starts to foam slightly.
- Whip the cream and gently mix the two preparations.
- Take a salad bowl (of height equal to its base).
- Coarsely crumble the meringues.
- Make layers by alternating the mixture (egg, sugar and whipped cream), meringue and caramel (start with the mixture and finish with the latter).
- Place this bowl in the freezer for about 6 hours and take it out in the middle of the meal.

Muffin-pudding
Serves 6

Preparation time: 10 min

Ingredients

2 muffins
50cl of milk

2 beaten eggs
50g sugar
1 tablespoon cocoa powder
1 apple

Preparation

Crumble the muffins.
Warm the milk and pour it over the muffins.
Add the cocoa powder.
Mix the eggs and the sugar and add them.
Dice the apple and add it.
Pour the mixture into a cake tin.
Bake for about an hour at 200°C (gas mark 7).
When the pudding starts to caramelize on top, cover it with aluminum foil and continue baking.

Hazelnut cupcakes with chocolate icing
Serves 8

Preparation time: 40 min

Ingredients

2 eggs
100g butter
50g of flour
60g hazelnut powder
100g of sugar
1/2 sachet of baking powder

Preparation

Preparation of the cake base:
Preheat your oven to 180°C.
Start by mixing the flour and the baking powder, then add the hazelnut powder,
the eggs and the sugar.
For the butter, work it first with your hands to make it soft and add it little
by little to the previous preparation for a homogeneous texture.
Butter your mold and pour the preparation into it and bake for 20 minutes.
For the butter cream:
In a bowl, mix the chocolate powder, powdered sugar, butter and milk (I advise
you to work it by hand for a better texture). When the mixture is homogeneous
and not too compact nor too liquid, place it in a piping bag (or freezer bag with
one of its corners cut off) and decorate your cupcakes out of the oven!
Then you can let your imagination run wild and decorate your cupcakes in any way you like!
Enjoy!

Light chocolate chip muffins

muffins: 14

Preparation time: 15 min

Ingredients

2 eggs
100g of chocolate chips
90g sugar
150g of white cheese0
20g of butter
300g of flour
1 packet of baking powder
2 tablespoons vanilla liquid
Milk

Preparation

Mix the eggs, vanilla and cottage cheese.
Add sugar, butter, baking powder, flour and grated chocolate (or chips).
If the dough is too compact, add milk to obtain a soft dough.
Pour the dough into muffin tins, filling them 2/3 full as they swell.
Put in the oven at thermostat 6 (180°C) for 20 to 30 minutes.

Madeleines maple butter
madeleines: 16

Preparation time: 15 min

Ingredients

2 eggs
100g of flour
1/2 sachet of yeast
70g of butter
30g of maple butter
70g of sugar

Preparation

Melt the butter in a saucepan until the butter smells nutty (almost boiling). Reserve it for later.
In a bowl, sift the flour with a bowl or a sieve, do the same with the yeast and the sugar.
For the eggs, separate the yolk from the white, then add the yolk
to the bowl along with the maple butter.
Beat the egg whites until stiff, then add them to the rest and mix.
Once the dough is homogeneous, add the butter.
Keep the dough in a cool place for 1 hour!
Divide the dough into the madeleine molds. Bake in the oven for about 15 minutes.
Advice:
- keep the dough in a cool place until you bake the second batch.

- If the silicone molds are new, it is better to use butter for the first use. If not, there is no need.

Carrot muffins with or without gluten
Muffins: 20

Preparation time: 15 min

Ingredients

2 eggs
100g brown or white sugar
100g sunflower oil (can be reduced)
250g of finely chopped carrots
170g wheat flour (or 90g cornflour + 90g cornflour for a gluten free recipe)
1 packet of baking powder (or 1 packet of baking powder for a gluten-free recipe)
1 teaspoon of cinnamon
1/2 teaspoon of ginger
50g of coconut milk

Preparation

Beat the 2 eggs with the sugar until the mixture turns white.
Add the oil and the grated carrots.
Add the sifted flour and yeast (or baking powder).
Spice with cinnamon and ginger.
Finish with the coconut milk.
Mix well and add candied fruits or nuts at the end of the preparation if you wish.
Fill small muffin tins and bake for about 20 minutes at 210°c.

coconut cookie with sprinkles
Serves 6

Preparation time: 10 min

Ingredients

2 eggs
100g of caster sugar
3 tablespoons of milk
4 tablespoons of peanut oil
1 tablespoon of rum
150g of flour
1 packet of baking powder
125g of grated coconut
100g of chocolate

Preparation

Mix everything according to the order of the ingredients. Put in the oven at Th 6 (180°C) for 50 mn.

Flambéed banana and nutella cupcakes

big cupcakes: 9

Preparation time: 20 min

Ingredients

2 eggs
110g melted butter
150g sugar
200g of flour
1 sachet of yeast
5cl of milk
2 ripe bananas
2 teaspoons brown sugar
2 rum
1 jar of nutella

Preparation

Prepare paper cases.
Start by frying your bananas in 10 g of butter. Add the brown sugar. When they are
well cooked, pour the rum and flambé. Mash the bananas well and set aside.
Preheat the oven to 180°C (gas mark 6).
In a bowl, mix the egg yolks and sugar. When the mixture is well whitened, add the flour and
the yeast. This makes a compact dough like crumble. Then add the milk and butter. Mix well.
Beat the egg whites until stiff and fold them into the mixture
gently. This will make your cakes lighter.
Finally, add the bananas.
Put the boxes in your muffin tin and add the mixture.
You can choose to make a nutella heart by filling halfway with batter then
adding a teaspoon of nutella and ending with the batter.
Bake for about 20 minutes.
Remove from oven and let cool before unmolding. Decorate the cupcake with the nutella.

My speculoos cupcakes

cupcakes about: 12

Preparation time: 40 min

Ingredients

2 eggs
120g of very soft butter (not melted!)
4 tablespoons of milk
140g of flour
100g powdered sugar

1 pinch of salt
2 teaspoons baking powder
1 pinch of powdered cinnamon (to flavour the dough according to taste)

Preparation

Start with the speculo dough if you make it yourself so that it has time to cool.
Otherwise, if you have chosen an industrial paste, go straight to the cake stage!
Place the speculoos on a sheet of parchment paper and bake them for
20 minutes in a preheated oven at 160° C (gas mark 5-6).
C (gas mark 5-6).
Then blend them in small batches to a fine powder.
In a saucepan, heat the milk, agave syrup and sugar (do not bring to the boil).
Put the cookie powder in a bowl, then pour half of the hot liquid over it and whisk vigorously.
The dough will become a little difficult to work with, so add the remaining liquid and mix.
Add the oil and mix again until the mixture is smooth. The speculoos dough is
still liquid, once it has cooled down, it will have the texture of a spread!
Pour it into a clean glass jar. Close it tightly and let it cool at room temperature
for a few minutes, then set it aside in the refrigerator.
For the cakes: preheat your oven to 180°C (gas mark 6).
Mix the soft butter and sugar in a bowl until the mixture whitens (it is important that the
butter is soft and not melted so that the cupcake dough is well aerated once it is cooked).
Add the eggs one by one, then the flour, salt, baking powder and cinnamon to taste!
Place paper (or silicone) cups in each cell of your muffin pan.
Place 2 tablespoons of batter in each cup (if there is too much batter, the cake will puff up and
overflow the pan), add a teaspoon of speculoos batter to each cake and bake for 20 minutes.
Meanwhile, prepare the frosting: whip the mascarpone with the liquid cream
and the speculoos paste (whip gently at first to avoid splashing!).
Once the cakes are cooked and cooled, you can frost them with a piping
bag or a spoon. Stick a speculo in each icing and enjoy!

Cupcakes all lemon
pieces: 10

Preparation time: 15 min

Ingredients

2 eggs
125g flour
125g melted butter
125g of sugar
1 cured lemon

Preparation

For the base:
Separate the egg whites and yolks.

Mix the melted butter and sugar in a bowl, add the egg yolks, then the
flour, and finally the juice of the lemon and its minced zest.
Beat the egg whites until stiff with a pinch of salt. Gently fold them into the mixture.
Bake in cupcake tins for 30 minutes at 150°C (gas mark 5). Check the cooking
with the tip of a knife.
Unmold the cupcakes when they are warm and let them cool completely.
For the icing:
In a saucepan, combine the lemon juice, sugar and whole egg. Whisk together
over low heat until set.
Cover cupcakes with cream, dipping tops directly into pan. Let cool.

Soft almond tuiles

Tiles: 10

Preparation time: 10 min

Ingredients

2 eggs
125g almond powder
75g of sugar
1 tablespoon of flour
Refined almonds

Preparation

In a bowl mix the eggs, almond powder, sugar and flour.
When the dough is compact, make medium sized balls.
Place the balls on a baking sheet lined with buttered aluminum foil.
The thicker the balls, the fluffier the tiles.
Place a few slivered almonds on each ball.
Bake for 10 to 15 minutes at 210 °C - TH 7, let cool and then remove the tiles!
With coffee or as a dessert with a custard it is delicious!

Lemon chocolate cupcakes

cupcakes: 12

Preparation time: 20 min

Ingredients

2 eggs
125g powdered sugar
125g of flour
1/2 sachet of yeast
125g of butter
1 tablespoon of lemon

Preparation

Preheat your oven to 180 °C (gas mark 6).
Place the paper cases in muffin tins.
In a bowl, beat together the sugar and eggs with an electric whisk until the mixture turns white.
Add the melted butter and lemon extract a little at a time while continuing to whisk.
Then gently fold in the yeast and flour.
Once your batter is smooth and even, fill the pans halfway, put them
in the oven halfway up and bake for about 15 minutes.
Allow to cool.
While the cakes are baking, prepare the frosting:
In a small saucepan, pour the lemon juice, sugar and egg white.
Whisk until mixture comes to a boil.
When the mixture boils, continue whisking for a few more minutes.
Remove from heat, add chocolate squares and mix until you have a smooth glaze.
Sprinkle the cupcakes with powdered sugar before coating them with the chocolate-lemon icing.
Decorate with sugar balls, chocolate sprinkles, marzipan...
Place in the refrigerator for at least 1 hour before eating.

Madeleine with hazelnut cream
madeleines: 16

Preparation time: 15 min

Ingredients

2 eggs
130g of flour with baking powder incorporated (or 130g of flour + 1/2 sachet of yeast)
130g of powdered sugar
65g hazelnut cream
65g of milk

Preparation

Preheat the oven to 240°C (gas mark 8).
Soften the hazelnut cream for 30 seconds in the microwave and
add the milk. Mix well until it is homogeneous.
In another bowl, beat the eggs.
Add flour, baking powder and sugar. Mix quickly.
Add the hazelnut cream.
Pour a tablespoon of batter into each cell of the buttered or oiled madeleine mold.
Bake in the middle of the oven for 4 minutes at 240°C, then lower the temperature
to 180°C for another 4 minutes. Do the same with the 2nd batch.
Turn out immediately and let the madeleines cool on a rack.

Cupcakes strawberry mascarpone
cupcakes: 12

Preparation time: 30 min

Ingredients

2 eggs
130g sugar
110g of flour
2 teaspoons of baking powder
2 tablespoons of oil
10cl of liquid cream
100g strawberry jam

Preparation

For the base:
Start by beating the two whole eggs with the sugar in a bowl.
Add the oil, then the cream.
Sift the flour with the yeast and incorporate it gently into the bowl.
Mix well to obtain a fairly fluid dough without lumps.
Preheat your oven to 170°C.
Line your cupcake pans with paper liners. Pour a tablespoon of batter into each one, then a spoonful of strawberry jam, and fill the rest of the mold with batter, up to 2 thirds.
When all the pans are filled, bake for 18 to 20 minutes.
For the glaze:
Pour the mascarpone and cream into a bowl.
For the fruity reminder, add a teaspoon of strawberry syrup, and about 4-5 drops of red dye to get a nice pale pink. Whip the mixture with a mixer or whisk, adding the powdered sugar little by little. You must obtain a perfectly homogeneous mixture.
Set the mixture aside in the refrigerator for half an hour before placing it (ideally with a piping bag) on your perfectly cooled cupcakes.

Spanish Madeleines (magdelenas)

Serves 6

Preparation time: 15 min

Ingredients

2 eggs
130g of sugar
12cl sunflower oil
70g of fresh cream (35% fat content)
175g of flour
1/2 sachet of baking powder
lemon or orange peel

Preparation

Preheat to 180°C (gas mark 6).
Put the muffin cases in the muffin tin.

Put the eggs and sugar in a bowl and beat with an electric whisk for 6 minutes.
Add the lemon zest and beat for 6 minutes.
Add oil and cream and mix for 3 minutes.
Add flour and yeast and mix for 20 seconds.
Let rest for 10 minutes.
Pour the dough into the cavities of the pan to 3/4 and sprinkle with sugar.
Bake for 20 minutes.

Lemon and Coconut Tart Muffins
pieces: 12

Preparation time: 20 min

Ingredients

2 eggs
150g sugar
400g of flour
5.5g of baking powder
100g butter (well softened)
100g of coconut powder
2bananas
2untreated lemon(s) (depending on your taste for acidity)

Preparation

In a bowl, mix the flour and the yeast with the coconut and the powdered sugar.
Add the butter, the 2 eggs (beaten with a few quick strokes of the fork) and a variable
amount of lemon zest. Mix again (the mixture remains quite floury).
Peel the fruit and cut into small pieces, add to the mixture with the lemon juice (the texture
should remain thick, but you can add a little water if needed to bind the mixture better).
Pour into prepared muffin cups, and again sprinkle with a mixture
of sugar and coconut, as desired.
Baking:
Place in a medium oven (200-220°C) for about 30 minutes.
Enjoy!

Chocolate, almond and chocolate chip muffins
muffins: 16

Preparation time: 10 min

Ingredients

2eggs
150g sugar
50g brown sugar
2 tablespoons cocoa powder
1 chocolate bar reduced to small pieces (or chips if you have them)

100g melted butter
Flaked almonds (as desired)

Preparation

Preheat the oven to 180°C (gas mark 6).
First, beat the eggs and sugar in a bowl and add the rest of the wet mixture.
Then, in a second dish, mix well the ingredients of the dry preparation.
The trick to this recipe is to mix the wet and dry mixes together
roughly (if there are lumps, so much the better).
Put the mixture in muffin tins and bake for 15-20 min at 180°C (gas mark 6).

raspberry muffins
muffins: 12

Preparation time: 10 min

Ingredients

2 eggs
150g sugar
50g brown sugar (or white sugar)
2 tablespoons raspberry or blackberry jam
100g melted butter
200g fresh or frozen raspberries

Preparation

In the first mixture, beat the eggs and sugar first, then add the rest of the ingredients.
Be careful when you add the raspberries: go easy on them, we're not making
a puree, they have to stay whole, as much as possible!
For the dry mixture, mix the flour and yeast well, that's all.
In one fell swoop (schplaf, yes: it's better to wear an apron, the raspberry
stains...), pour the wet mixture into the dry mixture.
And this is where the trick comes in: you don't stir, you mix roughly with a spoon and basta!
You don't try to get a smooth dough, there are lumps, it's normal. The dough is ugly,
it's normal (and there is not that the beauty which counts, moreover).
We pour this lumpy dough into muffin tins.
One puts in oven from 15 to 20 min to 180°C (thermostat 6).
The cooking time depends on the size and the material of your molds: in silicone
molds it cooks a little faster, and if the molds are small too.

Chocolate and praline shortbread cookies
pieces: 40

Preparation time: 30 min

Ingredients

2 eggs
150g of caster sugar
100g brown sugar
200g of soft butter
400g of flour
10g of yeast express
80g of praline
1 bar of dark chocolate (max 50%)

Preparation

Beat the 2 whole eggs with the sugar and brown sugar into a foam.
Add the flour previously mixed with the yeast and the softened butter. Add the praline.
The texture of the dough should be slightly sandy.
Roll out the dough to a height of 7 mm and use a mold to make small circles
and place them on a baking sheet.
Add your chocolate chips on top, taking care to insert them as little as possible.
Bake at 190° (thermostat 6-7) for about 8 minutes.

Madeleines of ririne
madeleines about: 25

Preparation time: 20 min

Ingredients

2 eggs
150g of caster sugar
150g of flour
125g melted butter
lemon zest
1/2 teaspoon of yeast

Preparation

Mix the eggs with the sugar. Whisk vigorously until the mixture is white.
Add the flour and the melted butter little by little. Incorporate the lemon zest, then the yeast.
Preheat oven to 210°C (gas mark 7).
Fill each cavity of a madeleine dish with a spoonful of dough. Bake in the oven for 10 minutes.
Remove the madeleines from the oven and unmould immediately.

Cinnamon and ginger madeleines
madeleines: 27

Preparation time: 15 min

Ingredients

2 eggs

150g of caster sugar
160g of flour
125 butter
2 teaspoons of cinnamon
2 teaspoons of ginger
1 sachet of yellow yeast

Preparation

Mix the eggs and sugar until you get a slightly foamy mixture.
Melt the butter.
Add the flour, yeast, warmed butter, cinnamon and ginger to the previous mixture.
Mix well with a wooden spoon.
Preheat oven to 210°C (gas mark 7).
Butter and flour the alveoli of a madeleine mold (unnecessary if the mold is made of silicone) then pour 1 teaspoon of the mixture into each alveoli.
Bake for 10 minutes.
Remove the madeleines from the oven and let them cool on parchment paper.

Muffins with jam
muffins: 12

Preparation time: 10 min

Ingredients

2 eggs
150g white sugar
50g brown sugar
Fruit jam (for my part, I have a preference for blueberry)
100g butter
250g of flour
1 sachet of yeast
1 pinch of salt

Preparation

In a dish, mix the eggs, white sugar and brown sugar.
Melt the butter and add it to the dish.
Add the flour, yeast and a pinch of salt.
Tip: add 1 to 2 tablespoons of blueberry jam to the batter to brown it and give it a subtle taste.
Pour a little batter into the muffin cups, then a small spoonful of jam, and cover with batter.
Bake for 20/25 minutes at 180°C (gas mark 6).

Mini muffins with banana peels
Serves 4

Preparation time: 10 min

Ingredients

2 eggs
150g sugar half white, half muscovado
180g of flour 1/2 white, 1/4 rye, 1/4 buckwheat
50g of butter
1 teaspoon of yeast
100g of water
3 organic banana peels

Preparation

Preheat your oven to 220° thermostat 7.
Place the banana peels in the bowl of a powerful blender. Add the water and turn on the maximum speed until you obtain a puree. It does not need to be smooth.
Mix your eggs with the butter and sugar until you have a clear, airy mixture.
Add the flour, yeast, and mashed banana peels and mix gently.
Butter mini-muffin tins and pour the mixture into them.
Bake for 15 minutes, and you're done!

Rose and white chocolate muffins

Serves 8

Preparation time: 20 min

Ingredients

2 eggs
180g of flour
100g cornflour
80g of sugar
1 sachet of vanilla sugar
80g of butter
1/2 sachet of baking powder
1 pinch of salt
10cl of milk
1 plain yogurt
20cl rose syrup
100g rose crystals
150g white chocolate

Preparation

Preheat your oven to 180°C (thermostat 6).
Prepare the first mixture of flour, cornflour, yeast and salt in a bowl.
Mix well and then add the crystallized rose petals and the white chocolate chips.
Prepare the second mixture.
In another bowl, whisk the eggs and then add the sugar and vanilla sugar. Mix well.
Melt the butter and add it to the mixture while continuing to stir.

Pour the milk and add the yogurt. Mix well and finish by pouring in the rose syrup.
Then add the first flour-maizen-yeast-salt mixture. Mix gently.
The dough should remain slightly lumpy.
Butter and flour the muffin tins and fill them 2/3 full with the mixture.
Bake for 20 minutes.

Carrot cupcakes with sweet and salty spices

cupcakes: 8

Preparation time: 45 min

Ingredients

2eggs
1carrot
120g flour
120g caster sugar
1 teaspoon baking powder
1 teaspoon cinnamon powder
2 pinches of ginger powder
1 vanilla bean (or vanilla flavoring)
1 pinch of cumin powder
6cl of oil
Food coloring (optional)

Preparation

Preheat your oven to 180°C (thermostat 6)
Peel, wash and grate the carrot. In a bowl, mix the flour, yeast, salt, cinnamon,
cumin and ginger powder.
Beat the eggs and brown sugar in another bowl until the mixture turns white. Split
the vanilla bean lengthwise, remove the seeds and add them to the mixture.
Whisk in oil until smooth.
Using a flexible spatula, stir in the flour and spice mixture, lifting the mixture
well. Then add the grated carrots and mix gently. You can add a little
food coloring to give your cakes a nice orange color.
Pour the batter into paper or muffin cases, preferably buttered. Bake in the oven
for 20 to 25 minutes. Take the cakes out of the oven and let them cool.
Meanwhile, in a bowl, pour the petits suisses and add the curry powder,
cumin and ras el hanout. Mix very gently so that the mixture does not become
liquid. Add food coloring to give a nice orange color.
When the cupcakes are cooled, transfer the preparation into a bag fitted with a fluted
tip and then on each cake, place a hat of cream and decorate with a carrot slice.
Let's get to work, rabbits, and enjoy!

Cinnamon cookies

Serves 5

Preparation time: 1h15

Ingredients

2 eggs
1 packet of vanilla sugar
1 pinch of salt
2 spoons of cinnamon
300g of flour
125g butter
125g almond powder
125g powdered sugar

Preparation

Preheat your oven to 180°C (thermostat 6).
Mix all the ingredients together.
Let your dough rest in the fridge for 1 hour.
Roll out the dough to a thickness of 5 cm and make shapes with cookie cutters.

Diet cookies
Serves 8

Preparation time: 30 min

Ingredients

2 eggs
1 cup of sugar tea
3/4 cup of neutral oil
1 packet of baking powder
1 pinch of baking soda
orange zest (or 2)
1 small handful of raisins
drop of vanilla liquid or 1 packet of vanilla sugar.
Flour on request

Preparation

- Zest the orange and set aside.
- Rinse the raisins and pat them dry. Set aside.
-Break the eggs in a bowl, add the sugar (+ vanilla sugar if necessary).
- Beat with a mixer for a few minutes.
- Add the oil and beat again.
- Add the yeast and bicarbonate (and liquid vanilla if necessary) and mix again.
- Add the zest and raisins.
- Then add the flour little by little.
- Mix first with a wooden spoon for a while.
- As the dough becomes more consistent, work it with your fingers.

- When the dough is soft and not sticky, roll it out with a rolling pin on a floured surface, on 1/2 cm thickness, and form cookies with a cookie cutter of your choice.
- Place on a baking sheet lined with baking paper. - Continue until the end of the dough.
- Bake for about 10/15 minutes, depending on the oven, the cookies should just take color.
- If you want crispy cookies, you can put them back in the oven still hot but turned off for a few more minutes.

Speculoos style shortbread
pieces: 40

Preparation time: 20 min

Ingredients

2 eggs
200g of butter
1 lemon peel
450g of flour
50g of cornflour
1 pinch of baking powder
150g powdered sugar
150g almond powder

Preparation

Mix flour, cornstarch, lemon zest and baking powder in a large bowl.
Cut the butter in small pieces and add them to the rest of the preparation
and work it with your fingertips.
Then add the sugar, eggs, almond powder and work the dough until it becomes soft.
Form the dough into a ball and roll it out. Let it rest in a cool place for 1h30.
Preheat the oven to 180°C (thermostat 6)
Then roll out the dough to a thickness of 4 mm and cut it out with cookie cutters.
Bake the shortbread on a tray covered with baking paper for 15 minutes.
Let them cool down and sprinkle them with powdered sugar.
Enjoy.

Breton muffins
large muffins: 10

Preparation time: 15 min

Ingredients

2 eggs
200g of flour
100g of salted butter or 1/2 salt + 20 g
15cl of milk (ribot is better)
180g of sugar

1/2 sachet of baking powder
2 apples
1 tablespoon of chouchen

Preparation

Preheat the oven to 200°C (thermostat 6-7).
Beat the eggs and sugar until frothy.
Melt the butter in the milk in a saucepan over low heat and pour
over the egg-sugar mixture while whisking.
Stir in flour and baking powder.
Dice the apples and brown them in 20 g of butter before adding
them to the batter with the chouchen.
Fill buttered and floured muffin tins and bake for 15 minutes.
The muffins are cooked when the blade of the knife stuck in the cakes comes out dry.

Chocolate and currant muffins
muffins: 10

Preparation time: 15 min

Ingredients

2 eggs
200g sugar
100g of chocolate
100g of butter
200g of currants
250g of flour
Yeast
Salt

Preparation

Preheat the oven to 180°C (thermostat 6).
First of all :
Melt the butter and chocolate in a saucepan.
Beat the eggs and sugar until the mixture whitens, then add the butter-chocolate
mixture and the currants.
In a second step:
Mix the flour, salt and baking powder.
Quickly add this mixture to the chocolate mixture and mix very gently with a wooden
spoon; but not too much, there must be a few lumps left for the muffins to puff up well!
Pour the mixture into the muffin tins and bake at 200°C (gas mark
6-7), then at 180°C (gas mark 6) for 20 minutes.
Check the cooking with a knife blade.

Double chocolate heart cookie

Serves 6

Preparation time: 40 min

Ingredients

2 eggs
200g brown sugar
80g of sugar
220g of butter
350g of flour
1 sachet of yeast
salt
60g of peanut butter
50g of dark chocolate
12 teaspoons of chocolate spread

Preparation

On a sheet of baking paper, place 12 teaspoons of spread. Set aside in a cool place.
In a bowl, combine the sugars and soft butter. Add eggs and whisk again.
Add flour, baking powder and salt. Mix.
Divide the dough in two. Add 60g of peanut butter to one half, and the melted
dark chocolate to the other half. Mix well until completely incorporated.
Place each of the preparations in cling film, flatten slightly and set aside in the fridge for 1 hour.
Flour your work surface and roll out the peanut butter dough
into a not too thin rectangle. Set aside.
Do the same with the chocolate dough and place it on the previous dough.
Cut the rectangle in 2. Take one part and fold it in half. Roll out again into a
rectangle and then roll up the whole lengthwise, pressing it tightly. Do not hesitate
to flour your work surface regularly, your dough should never stick.
Cut out pieces of 1-2cm each and roll them out in a circle on your floured work surface.
Stop when the size suits you, but be careful, the cookies will spread when cooked!
Take your spread from the fridge and place a portion in the center of 12
cookies. Close with a second cookie circle. Weld and place on a baking
sheet lined with parchment paper. Repeat for all cookies.
Bake for 13 minutes at 180 degrees.

Chocolate cookies

Serves 8

Preparation time: 30 min

Ingredients

2 eggs
200g brown sugar
150g of caster sugar
1 spoonful of vanilla extract

450g of flour
1 sachet of baking powder
200g of butter
1 pinch of salt
100g of chocolate

Preparation

Beat the eggs, vanilla and 2 sugars in a bowl until the mixture becomes frothy. Add the flour and sifted yeast, salt, then the melted butter, working well with a wooden spatula to avoid lumps. Add the chocolate chips to the dough without overworking it. Lightly oil a baking sheet, place small piles of dough (30 g) on top. Put in a cool place until you preheat the oven to Th 6 or 180°C. Bake at half height and let cook 10 minutes per plate (for indication, the cookie must have a browner border on the edge of the cake than its center and be tender and soft in its heart. Once baked, place them one by one on a wire rack to cool completely.

Lemon Raspberry Cupcakes
pieces: 12

Preparation time: 45 min

Ingredients

2 eggs
20cl of milk
150g of flour
150g of cornflour
1 pack of yeast
120g of brown sugar
125g melted butter
1 pinch of salt
1 teaspoon of lemon flavouring
150g of raspberries

Preparation

Decorate with colored pearls.
Preheat the oven to 200°C (thermostat 6-7).
Pour the flour, cornstarch and yeast into a bowl. Mix, then form a well.
Add the eggs and milk gradually, add the brown sugar, melted butter and lemon and mix until you have a smooth dough.
Pour the batter into small molds, scatter 3 to 4 raspberries on top of each mold and bake at 200°C (thermostat 6-7) for 20 to 25 minutes.
Allow to cool.
Meanwhile, make the glaze:
Crush the softened butter with a fork, then gradually add, alternately, the powdered sugar and jelly, then the milk.

Whisk the mixture until you obtain the icing.
Unmould the cakes, add the icing with a spatula and carefully pour the coloured pearls or other sweet decorations on top.

chocolate chip muffins
Muffins: 12

Preparation time: 20 min

Ingredients

2 eggs
2 teaspoons vanilla liquid
75g melted butter
25cl of liquid cream
350g of flour
1/2 sachet of baking powder
1 pinch of salt
115g of caster sugar
75g of chocolate

Preparation

In a bowl, mix the eggs + the liquid vanilla + the melted butter + the fresh cream.
Mix well.
Add flour + baking powder + salt + sugar + chips.
Preheat the oven to 200°C (thermostat 6-7) for 10 min.
Fill the moulds to 2/3.
Bake for 15 min.

Banana cupcake
cupcakes: 10

Preparation time: 15 min

Ingredients

2 eggs
40g butter (melted)
90g of flour
1 pinch of salt
45g of sugar
1 teaspoon of yeast
3 bananas
1 tablespoon of milk
Chocolate spread for the glaze

Preparation

Mix the eggs and sugar, preferably with a whisk. The mixture will become a bit frothy and white.
Add the milk, flour, melted butter, yeast and salt.
The dough is homogeneous. Finally add the mashed bananas.
Pour in the moulds, maximum to the 2/3.
Put in the oven for 20 min at 180°C (thermostat 6), the inside will remain soft (not cooked).
Then, glaze with chocolate spread before eating.

Banana-chocolate-praline muffins
muffins: 20

Preparation time: 10 min

Ingredients

2 eggs
50g of butter
20cl of liquid cream
10 tablespoons of flour
8 tablespoons of powdered sugar
1 sachet of baking powder
1banana
100g of chocolate
100g of praline
1 pinch of salt

Preparation

Preheat the oven to 180°C (thermostat 6).
Melt the butter.
In a bowl, mix the flour, sugar and yeast.
Make a well and add the eggs, melted butter and cream.
Mix well until you obtain a homogeneous paste.
Add the chocolate chips and the praline.
Mix well.
Cut the banana into small cubes (not too fine so that they don't get crushed when
you mix them into the batter). Add them to the batter and mix gently.
Fill muffin tins 3/4 full.
Bake in the oven for about 15 minutes (time may vary by a few minutes depending
on the type of oven).
Remove from oven and let cool.
Unmould the muffins.
Enjoy.

Light apple, quince and chocolate muffins
muffins: 6

Preparation time: 15 min

Ingredients

2 eggs
50g flour
50g almond powder
1 packet of baking powder
100g of sugar (I replace it with 2 tablespoons of liquid sweetener because of my diabetes)
1 plain yogurt
100g of quince compote (can be replaced by any compote according to the desired taste)
6 squares of dark chocolate

Preparation

Beat the eggs with the sugar.
Add the flour, almond powder and yeast.
Mix in the plain yoghurt and the chosen compote.
Preheat the oven to 180° (thermostat 6).
Pour half of the preparation into muffin tins.
Place the chocolate square in the muffin (you can cut it in 2 to double the chocolate area in the muffin).
Pour the rest of the preparation.
Bake for 15/20min depending on the power of your oven. Watch with the tip of the knife, as soon as it is dry, take it out of the oven. (15min top chrono with my oven)
Very soft muffins thanks to the compote.
No butter and no sugar, so no complexes!

Soft cinnamon madeleines
madeleines: 15

Preparation time: 10 min

Ingredients

2 eggs
50g of sugar
50g of flour
20g cornstarch
60g of butter
1/2 sachet of yeast
1 tablespoon of cinnamon powder

Preparation

Preheat your oven to 200°C (thermostat 6-7).
Mix the sugar and the eggs until the mixture is frothy, then add the melted butter and mix again until you get a smooth mixture. Add the flour, cornstarch and yeast and mix vigorously until you have a nice smooth dough.
Add a tablespoon of cinnamon powder and mix well. Let the

dough rest for 5 to 10 minutes in a cool place.
Meanwhile, butter and flour the madeleine molds.
Place the dough in the molds and bake for 13-15 minutes (depending on the oven).
It's ready!

Owl cupcakes for Halloween
cupcakes: 6

Preparation time: 25 min

Ingredients

2 eggs
60g dark dessert chocolate
50g of butter
40g sugar
25g of flour

Preparation

Preheat the oven to 180°C (thermostat 6).
For the cake base:
In a food processor or large bowl, whisk the eggs with the sugar until they turn white.
Melt the butter with the chocolate for a few seconds in the microwave.
Add this mixture to the rest of the mixture. Mix again.
Add the flour a little at a time and mix well.
Put the dough in mini silicone molds or baking trays, making sure to fill them 3/4 of the way.
Bake for about 25 minutes at 180 °C (gas mark 6). Keep an eye on the cooking time.
Let your cakes cool on a wire rack.
For the icing :
Mix the Oreo cookies with a blender.
Mix the cold mascarpone with the mixed Oreos and powdered sugar.
Put in a piping bag, frost your cupcakes, making sure to keep a smooth surface
to hold the owl decoration on top.
For the owl decoration:
For the owl's eyes, place two halves of oreo on the icing side by side (making sure to keep the
white icing inside) In the middle of each half of oreo: place a brown smartie to make the eye.
Finish by making the nose: to do this, place a smartie in the middle
of the two halves of the oreo, vertically, in orange.
Your owls are ready!

Madeleines with praline and pink icing
small madeleines: 25

Preparation time: 10 min

Ingredients

2 eggs

70g of sugar
1/2 sachet of yeast
150g of flour
70g of butter
10cl of milk
2 teaspoons vanilla bourbon
2 tablespoons of praline paste
50g of praline
g of almond powder

Preparation

Preheat the oven to 220°C.
Melt the praline paste in the milk over low heat.
Mix the eggs and sugar.
Add the milk + praline paste mixture.
Incorporate the melted butter, yeast, flour, praline powder and bourbon vanilla.
Add the almond powder.
The dough should be quite dry and compact. If necessary you can add more almond powder.
Put the dough in the madeleine molds and bake for 10 minutes.
Once the madeleines have cooled, prepare your icing.
Melt the white chocolate with the butter.
Remove from the heat and add the powdered sugar, orange blossom water and coloring.
Using a brush, apply a thin layer of icing on the madeleines.
You can add decoration, sugar crystals etc.

Apple Madeleines
pieces: 8

Preparation time: 20 min

Ingredients

2 eggs
75g of flour
75g of butter
1 tablespoon of honey
1 tablespoon of powdered sugar
1/4 sachet of baking powder
2 apples

Preparation

Soften the butter. Mix all the ingredients - except the apples - in a bowl. Peel and cut the apples in 8.
Put 2 pieces of apple in muffin tins, then a tablespoon of batter in each tin.
Bake for 45 minutes at 150°C (gas mark 5).

Cupcakes and light icings

pieces approx.: 10

Preparation time: 20 min

Ingredients

2 eggs
75g sugar
120g of flour
1 sachet of yeast
100g of butter
100g of milk chocolate

Preparation

Preparation of the cake :
Preheat your oven to 180°C (thermostat 6).
Melt the butter and chocolate together in a bain-marie.
In the meantime, beat the eggs and sugar with a whisk and add the flour and a little yeast.
Add the chocolate and melted butter to the mixture.
Fill each mold (caissette) to 2/3 and bake for about 15/20 min.
Preparation of the icing:
Mix the small fresh cheese with the powdered sugar. Mix well.
If you want several colors of icing, divide the mixture into as many containers as you want.
Add a few drops of coloring to each container.
Fill frostings into piping bags (you can use freezer bags by placing all the frosting
in one corner and folding the other corner) and place in the refrigerator.
Dressing:
After letting the cakes cool, remove the bags from the refrigerator and top the cakes
with them. You can add small decorations to make them even more appetizing!
Enjoy!

fruity madeleines
madeleines: 16

Preparation time: 20 min

Ingredients

2 eggs
80g of flour
1/2 sachet of baking powder
80g of brown sugar
80g of salted butter
1/2golden apple
1 handful of raisins
Apricotsecs
Grated coconut

Preparation

Melt the butter and let it cool. In a bowl, mix the flour, yeast and sugar. Break the eggs, separating the whites from the yolks. Add the yolks to the mixture. Lightly whisk the whites without beating them and then add them. Pour in the melted butter and mix briskly with a whisk. Peel the apple and cut it into small cubes, add them to the batter along with the raisins, apricots in small pieces and coconut. Pour this preparation into madeleine molds or paper cases and bake for about 20 minutes in a hot oven.

Small sweet muffins apple lemon
small muffins: 20

Preparation time: 10 min

Ingredients

2 eggs
80g sugar
100g of flour
1/2 sachet of yeast
1 yogurt
3 tablespoons sunflower oil
2apples (Canadian)
1 cured lemon

Preparation

Preheat oven to 180°C (thermostat 6).
Beat the eggs in omelette and add the sugar. Mix well with a whisk. Add successively the sifted flour, the yeast, the yogurt and the oil. Mix well again. Finally, add the 2 peeled and diced apples and zest the lemon. Mix well.
Fill the muffin tins and bake for about 20 minutes until the muffins are puffed and golden.

Madeleines with m&m's
Madeleines: 12

Preparation time: 10 min

Ingredients

2 eggs
90g of powdered sugar
100g of flour
1 teaspoon of baking powder
100g of butter
1/2 teaspoon vanilla powder
65g of peanut M&M's

Preparation

In a bowl, mix the flour and the baking powder with the butter.
Add the eggs and sugar and mix well.
Crush 50 g of m&m's, add them to the dough with the vanilla.
Preheat oven to 220°C (gas mark 7-8).
Put the dough in the refrigerator for 15 minutes.
Divide the dough between the cavities of a madeleine mold and sprinkle with a little m&m's.
Place in the oven and bake for 8 minutes, then lower the oven temperature
to 180°C (gas mark 6) and bake for about 10 minutes.

Ginger cookies
Serves 4

Preparation time: 20 min

Ingredients

2 eggs (whites and yolks separated)
50g powdered sugar + 20g to sprinkle on the cookies
35g of powdered sugar
45g of flour
40g cornstarch
1 sachet of baking powder
25g whipped cream
75g candied ginger (finely chopped)
1 pinch of salt
Parchment paper

Preparation

Beat the yolks with the powdered sugar until the mixture swells.
Mix flour, cornstarch and baking powder. Stir the mixture into the yolks.
Beat egg whites with salt until stiff. As soon as they start to stiffen, add the powdered
sugar while continuing to beat. Gently fold into the previous mixture.
Line the baking sheet with parchment paper. Using a pastry bag,
pipe 24 small piles of dough into the pan.
Cook for 7 to 8 minutes in a 210°C (th.6) oven. Let cool before removing from the baking sheet.
Mix ginger and whipped cream. Garnish the flat side with 12 cookies. Place remaining
cookies on top. Sprinkle with powdered sugar and enjoy.

Nutella Praline Muffins
muffins: 9

Preparation time: 10 min

Ingredients

2 eggs
120g of butter + a little for the moulds

1 jar of plain yogurt
240g of chocolatepraline
100g of nutella
9 hazelnuts for decoration (optional)
200g of flour
1 packet of baking powder
150g of powdered sugar

Preparation

Preheat the oven to 180°C (th. 6).
In a saucepan, melt the butter and the praline chocolate cut into pieces, then set aside.
Lightly butter the muffin tins to make them easier to remove from
the moulds or line each one with a paper tray.
In a bowl or food processor, beat sugar and eggs until light and fluffy.
Add the flour and baking powder, then pour in the yogurt and melted butter to soften the dough.
Mix to obtain a smooth and homogeneous dough.
Using a spoon, fill the moulds two-thirds full.
Bake for 20 minutes, until the muffins are puffed, golden on the outside and cooked on the inside.
Check for doneness with the tip of a knife: it should come out dry.
Remove the muffins from the oven and let them cool on a rack.
Using a piping bag fitted with a fluted tip, decorate the muffins with a small
dome of Nutella, place a hazelnut on top, and enjoy without waiting.

Light orange cookie
Serves: 6

Preparation time: 20 min

Ingredients

2 untreated oranges + 1 optional
3 eggs
5 tablespoons of flour
3 tablespoons cornstarch
3 tablespoons of sugar
1/2 sachet of yeast
2 tablespoons of powdered sugar

Preparation

Preheat the oven to 200°C (thermostat 6-7).
Rinse 2 oranges, peel one and squeeze both into separate glasses; set aside.
Separate the whites from the yolks. Beat whites until stiff with a pinch of salt.
Mix yolks with flour, cornstarch, sugar, baking powder, zest and juice of one orange.
Gently fold the egg whites into the mixture.
Place the mixture in a lightly oiled non-stick (or silicone) 20 cm diameter
mold and bake for 20 to 30 minutes.

Meanwhile, prepare a topping:
In a small saucepan, dilute the juice of the second orange with the 2 tablespoons of confectioners' sugar, heat over medium heat and remove from the gas as soon as it starts to boil.
Turn the cake out of the pan and cover with the warm glaze.
Optional:
Peel the third orange and slice it thinly. Decorate the top of the cake with these slices and serve.

Tea Cookie Praline
Serves 8

Preparation time: 30 min

Ingredients

2 packages of tea cookies
180g of sugar
75g of butter
125g of praline powder (or hazelnuts)
125g dark chocolate
1 glass of coffee

Preparation

Melt the butter and chocolate in the microwave.
Add the sugar and the powdered pralines and mix well.
Dip the cookies in the coffee.
In a cake tin, alternate a layer of cookies and a layer of chocolate-praline cream.
Place in the refrigerator overnight.

Verrines of tiramisu with pears and speculoos
Serves 6

Preparation time: 25 min

Ingredients

2 packages of crushed speculoos cookies (about 400 g) (keep some whole for assembly)
100g sugar
5 eggs
2 packets of vanilla sugar
500g of mascarpone
1 can of leek syrup
5cl of pear liqueur
Bitter cocoa (about 3 teaspoons)
1 pinch of salt

Preparation

Dice the pears, add 1 sachet of vanilla sugar and a little pear liqueur and leave to macerate.

Separate the egg whites from the yolks.
Mix the yolks with the sugar, the remaining vanilla sugar and the mascarpone.
Beat the egg whites with a pinch of salt.
Fold into the first preparation.
Assemble in verrines: place a layer of crushed speculoos, then a layer of mascarpone
and the diced pears.
Break a few speculoos in half and before finishing, insert them into the verrines.
Finish with a layer of mascarpone.
Put a thin layer of bitter cocoa and leave in the refrigerator for at least 5 or 6 hours or more.

Tiramisu with speculoos, chocolate chips and honey
Serves 6

Preparation time: 15 min

Ingredients

2 packages of Bruges speculoos
100g of sugar
3 eggs
1 sachet of vanilla sugar
500g of mascarpone
Coffee or chocolate powder
Honey
Chocolate or pastry chocolate
Bitter cocoa

Preparation

Separate the whites from the yolks.
Mix the yolks with the sugar and mascarpone.
Beat the egg whites until stiff.
Add to the first preparation.
Cut out nuggets or take ready-made ones and pour them into the batter.
Take a square dish.
Alternate a layer of speculoos dipped in cold chocolate milk or coffee,
a layer of mascarpone and a drizzle of honey.
Fill the dish and finish with a layer of mascarpone.
Put a thin layer of bitter cocoa and leave in a cool place for at least 5 or 6 hours.

Galette des rois almond cream-speculoos
Serves 10

Preparation time: 20 min

Ingredients

2 flaky pastries pure butter

90g of almonds
90g of butter
90g brown sugar
200g of speculoos cream (from the spread section)
2 eggs + 1 yolk
1/2 teaspoon of cinnamon
1 bean

Preparation

In a bowl, mix the sugar and almond powder.
Add the softened butter, then work by hand to obtain a homogeneous almond paste.
Add the eggs one by one, then the speculoos cream and finally the cinnamon.
Unroll a puff pastry on a baking sheet.
Spread the almond cream with speculoos on top, leaving 2 cm on the edges.
Brush these 2 cm with egg yolk diluted in a teaspoon of water.
Place the bean in the almond cream with speculoos.
Cover with the second puff pastry, pinching the edges so that they seal together.
Draw patterns with the tip of a knife, then brush the cake with egg yolk.
Bake in a preheated oven at 220°C for 30 minutes.

Chocolate pear trifle with macaroons
Serves: 2

Preparation time: 30 min

Ingredients

2 pears
2 eggs (yolks)
50g powdered sugar
100g of mascarpone
1 teaspoon jasmine flower water
6 chocolate macaroons
10cl of liquid cream

Preparation

Whip the cream in a cold bowl.
When it is thick, add the mascarpone and mix well.
Whisk the 2 egg yolks with the 35g of sugar and make it white.
Add to the previous mixture (cream and mascarpone).
Add 2 drops of jasmine flower water.
Mix one last time before setting aside in the refrigerator.
Make the syrup: gently heat 20 cl of water with 20 g of sugar and 3 drops of jasmine flower water.
Peel the pears and cut them into small cubes.
Sprinkle them with the slightly cooled syrup and mix well.
Set aside in a cool place.

For the presentation:
in a pretty glass, alternate layers of pears, mascarpone cream and broken macaroons to taste.

Pear with chocolate, schnapps and specula
Serves 3

Preparation time: 10 min

Ingredients

2 pears
Pear schnapps
100g dark chocolate
20cl of fresh cream
3 peculiar cakes

Preparation

Peel and dice the pears and place them in a glass or bowl.
Add a few drops of schnapps on the pears.
Melt the chocolate squares in a double boiler and add the fresh cream.
Once the chocolate has melted, add it to the pears.
Crumble the speculoos and sprinkle over the chocolate.

light pear muffins
Serves 6

Preparation time: 10 min

Ingredients

2 pears
1 half wheat bran
1 half of oats
1 packet of vanilla sugar
1 teaspoon aspartame
1 teaspoon yeast
1 pinch of salt
1egg
2 teaspoons olive oil
Raisins for decoration (optional)

Preparation

Peel the pears and chop them finely without making a mush.
Mix all ingredients together.
Put in a muffin tin and place some raisins on top.
Cook for about 5 minutes in the microwave at 700 W.
Let cool a little and remove from the pan.

To taste.

Gluten free pear frangipane muffins
muffins: 10

Preparation time: 20 min

Ingredients

2 Comice type pears (or 4 small Williams type)
150g of butter + 10g for the moulds
80g sugar (preferably unrefined)
50g of honey (rather liquid)
125g almond powder
3 eggs
130g cornstarch
70g gluten free flour (rice, chestnut or mix)
1 sachet of yeast (or 1/2 if you prefer muffins that are a little more packed)
2 tablespoons of amaretto or rum (or 1 spoon of each)

Preparation

Combine sugar, honey and eggs. Beat for a few minutes.
Add the soft butter and mix well.
Mix the cornstarch, flour and baking powder. Add to the mixture and mix well again.
Add the Amaretto (or rum).
Peel the pears, cut them into pieces and add them to the mixture.
Preheat oven to 160°C (gas mark 5-6).
Butter 10 muffin tins and fill four-fifths with the mixture.
Bake for 35 minutes at 160°C (the tip of a knife should come out dry, otherwise continue baking for 10 minutes).

Tiramisu with caramelized apples and speculoos
Serves 2

Preparation time: 45 min

Ingredients

2 apples
1 sachet of vanilla sugar
50g of butter
100g of sugar
1 pinch of cinnamon

Preparation

Peel and dice the 2 apples, and put the 50 g of butter in a saucepan over low heat and add the apples. Let them brown a little and add the vanilla sugar

and the 100 g of sugar. Let it caramelize and keep it in the fridge.
Put the 250 g of mascarpone in a bowl with the vanilla sugar and the 100 g of sugar. Separate the yolks from the egg whites. Add the 2 egg yolks to the preparation and beat until you have a smooth cream. Leave it aside and beat the egg whites to obtain a kind of mousse. Add it delicately to the cream and put the bowl in the fridge. Crumble some speculoos, set aside. Make a liquid caramel and cut the speculoos in half by soaking them in caramel. Arrange the cake with a layer of speculoos, caramelized apples and mascarpone. Repeat this as many times as you like and finish by sprinkling with the crumbled speculoos and adding a caramelized speculoos as a decoration.
Leave in the fridge for at least 3-4 hours and then enjoy!

Caramelized apple cookie
Serves 4

Preparation time: 20 min

Ingredients

2apples
4 egg yolks
6 egg whites
200g sugar
50g of butter
80g of flour

Preparation

Beat the egg whites until they are not too stiff, add 20g of sugar at the end.
Whip the yolks with 80g of sugar, add the sifted flour and then incorporate the egg whites.
Melt the rest of the sugar until you obtain a blond caramel and add the butter.
Pour the caramel into a round mould and place the apple slices at the bottom of the mould. Cover with the cookie.
Bake at thermostat 5-6 (170°C) for 25 minutes.

Baked apples stuffed with speculoos
Serves 2

Preparation time: 25 min

Ingredients

2 apples (Royal Gala type for example)
3 speculoos
1 knob of butter
1 pinch of cinnamon (optional)
2 tablespoons brown sugar (or sugar)

Preparation

Wash and rinse apples (without peeling).
Cut a cap from each apple.
Scoop out the apples with an apple corer or a small spoon.
Preheat oven to 210°C (gas mark 7).
Crush the speculoos (with a blender, or by putting them in a plastic
bag and crushing with a rolling pin).
Mix them with the butter with your fingertips until you have a coarse paste.
Stuff the apples with the mixture and sprinkle with brown sugar and cinnamon.
Place the apples in a baking dish, and place the caps in the dish next to the apples.
Put 3 or 4 tablespoons of water in the bottom of the dish (to prevent
the juice from burning), and bake for 20 minutes.
Serve, putting the caps back on the apples.

Caramelized apple and chocolate cupcakes
cupcakes: 10

Preparation time: 40 min

Ingredients

2golden apples
125g butter
140g caster sugar
2 medium or large eggs
1 teaspoon vanilla extract
110g flour
1/2 sachet of yeast
15cl of milk
50cl of liquid cream
150g of dark chocolate

Preparation

Preparation of the cake:
Preheat the oven to 180°C (thermostat 6).
Peel and cut the apples into small pieces. Brown them in 15 g of butter and sprinkle
with 30 g of brown sugar. Leave to brown over low heat (about 8 - 10 minutes).
While the apples are slowly caramelizing, prepare the cake base.
Put the butter in a bowl. Work it until it is soft. Add sugar, eggs, vanilla extract,
baking powder, flour and milk. Mix well until the dough is smooth.
Divide batter among paper or silicone cups or directly into a muffin pan if you don't have one. Fill
the pans only three-quarters full to prevent the cakes from becoming too puffy after baking.
Add 4 or 5 apple pieces per cupcake.
Bake for about 15 minutes.
Once baked, let cool.
Preparation of the icing:
Heat the crème fraiche in a saucepan. Break the chocolate into small pieces in a bowl. Pour the

boiling cream over the chocolate and mix until you obtain a smooth and shiny glaze. Let cool.
Next, dip the top of each cupcake into the icing, holding it by its case.
Drain and flip. Now all you have to do is decorate.
You can then let your imagination run wild: almond petals, raspberries,
sugar pearls... all the originality is allowed!

Galette des rois macaron style
Serves 6

Preparation time: 30 min

Ingredients

2 rolls of puff pastry
100g powdered sugar
100g of almonds
1 egg yolk + 1 yolk to seal the edges
25g of butter
1 tablespoon of rum
drop of almonds
1 bean

Preparation

Prepare the almond cream by mixing the almond powder, the sugar, the whole egg
and the 25 gr of melted butter, the rum and the drops of bitter almond.
Place a disk of puff pastry on the baking sheet of the oven, pricked with the tip of a knife.
After obtaining a nice cream, place it on the puff pastry disk, leaving
a 3 cm border that will be brushed with egg yolk.
Do not forget the bean.
Place the second disc of pastry, sealing the edges well.
Chisel the edges with a sharp knife.
PREPARE THE MACAROON CRUST
Mix sugar, almond powder and egg whites.
Spread on the cake.
Bake for 30 minutes at 180°, the crust will become golden.
Serve warm.
Enjoy.

Verrine of snickers cream with speculoos
Serves 2

Preparation time: 5 min

Ingredients

2snickers
1 pint of light liquid cream
1/2 leaf gelatin

5 speculoos

Preparation

Soak the 1/2 sheet of gelatine in cold water to soften it.
In a saucepan, heat the cream and add the 2 snickers cut into pieces, stirring regularly.
Once the snickers have melted, add the gelatin (after draining it) and stir again.
Let cool a little (I put the bottom of my pan in cold water to speed up)
Coarsely crush the speculoos in the bottom of the verrines (2 and a half per verrine) and add the warm preparation.
Put in the fridge for at least 4 hours and enjoy.

Small coconut and speculoos flans

Serves 4

Preparation time: 15 min

Ingredients

2 speculoos
60g of grated coconut
2 eggs
70g brown sugar
lemon zest
25cl of milk
100g caster sugar (for the caramel)
2cl water (for the caramel)

Preparation

Prepare the caramel by pouring the sugar and water into a saucepan.
Place over medium heat until the mixture turns golden.
Pour the hot caramel into four small ovenproof ramekins and let cool.
Mix the cookies into a powder, mix with the grated coconut and set aside. Preheat oven to 180°C (th.5).
Beat the eggs, brown sugar and lemon zest until frothy. Add the milk and mix. Then, lastly, the preparation biscuits-coconut. Mix again.
Pour into the ramekins.

Kourambiedes (Greek Christmas and New Year cookies)

Serves: 6

Preparation time: 20 min

Ingredients

2 cups of butter
2 egg yolks
3 cups of flour

1 cup of sugar
1 cup of powdered sugar
1 teaspoon of baking powder
1/2 cup of cognac
1/2 teaspoon baking soda
1 cup of toasted almonds
Orange blossom water at discretion

Preparation

Let the butter soften and beat in a mixer for 15 minutes until it turns white.
Then add the yolks, sugar, bicarbonate, yeast, cognac, almonds and finally
the flour little by little until you get a fairly tight dough.
Let rest for 1 hour in a warm place, covered with a cloth.
Shape the dough into egg-sized balls or a more traditional crescent shape.
Put in a buttered oven dish and cook (Th 6 - 180°C) 15 to 20 min.
After removing from the oven, sprinkle with orange blossom and lots of sifted powdered sugar.

Raspberry and white chocolate muffins
muffins: 12

Preparation time: 15 min

Ingredients

2 cups of flour
1/2 cup powdered sugar
1 tablespoon baking powder
1/4 teaspoon of salt
1 egg
1 cup of milk
1/4 cup of oil
1 cup of raspberries
1 cup of white chocolate

Preparation

Mix the first 4 ingredients in a bowl.
Mix the next 3 ingredients in another dish, then mix them with the first ones.
Add raspberries and white chocolate.
Fill 12 muffin cups with paper liners.
Bake for 25 minutes at 190°C (gas mark 6-7).

Soft pineapple muffins
muffins: 20

Preparation time: 20 min

Ingredients

2 cups of flour
1 teaspoon baking powder
1/2 teaspoon baking soda
1 pinch of salt
60g of butter
1/2 cup of brown sugar
1 egg
1 cup of plain cottage cheese
1 small can of pineapple, with juice
1/4 cup of milk
1 teaspoon vanilla liquid
Powdered sugar

Preparation

Preheat the oven to 180°C, thermostat 6, grease the muffin tins.
Mix together the dry ingredients in a bowl.
In another bowl, beat butter and sugar, add egg, cottage cheese, vanilla extract, milk and 1/4 cup
of the juice from the pineapple can (keep the rest for the icing), then the pineapple in small pieces.
Pour the contents of the second bowl into the first, mix without insisting
(there should be lumps, and stirring too much will cause the batter to fall
out), divide between the pans and bake for about 20 minutes.
Remove from the oven and let cool in the molds for 10 minutes before removing
from the molds onto a rack.
Once the muffins have cooled, you can make a glaze: put a few tablespoons of powdered sugar
in a bowl and add pineapple juice in small quantities until you reach the desired consistency.
Put the icing in a small freezer bag, cut a tiny opening in one corner and drizzle
over the top of the cooled cakes.

Delicious Chocolate Chip Muffins
Serves 14

Preparation time: 1 hour

Ingredients

2 cups flour
2 tablespoons instant yeast
1/4 spoon of bicarbonate
1/2 spoon of salt
2 cups of chocolate (or a mixture of dark and/or white chocolate chips)
160g butter
1/2 cup of white and/or brown sugar
2 spoons of vanilla
3 eggs
250ml of milk

Preparation

Preheat oven to 190°C or 370°F (thermostat 6).
Mix the flour, instant yeast, baking soda and salt in a bowl.
In another bowl, mix the chocolate chips with a tablespoon of the flour mixture.
In a third bowl, mix the butter with an electric whisk on medium power for 3 minutes
until fluffy. Add the sugar and mix. Add the vanilla extract and eggs one at a time.
Continue to mix gently and alternately add the flour mixture
(in 3 batches) and the milk (in 2 batches).
Finally add the chocolate chips to the mixture and divide the batter
into the buttered and floured muffin cups.
Bake in the preheated oven for 30 minutes or until a knife inserted
in the center of the muffin comes out clean.
Place the pan on a baking sheet and let cool for at least 20 minutes. Unmould
your muffins and enjoy! :)

Ginger Cookies
cookies: 12

Preparation time: 15 min

Ingredients

2 cups of flour
2 teaspoons baking soda
2 teaspoons ground ginger
1/2 teaspoon ground cinnamon
1 pinch of salt
1/4 cup candied ginger
3/4 cup of sugar
3/4 cup of oil
1/4 cup molasses
1/4 cup maple syrup
1egg

Preparation

1) Cut the candied ginger in small pieces.
2) Mix in a bowl: flour, bicarbonate, ginger, cinnamon and salt.
3) Mix in another bowl the rest of the ingredients.
4) Gradually add the dry ingredients. Use a wooden spoon.
5) Shape the dough into 12 balls and roll them in the granulated sugar.
6) Place on 2 cookie sheets and bake, one at a time, at 180ºC for 15 minutes.

Macaroons
Serves 4

Preparation time: 10 min

Ingredients

2 cups of oatmeal
1 cup of sugar
1 egg

Preparation

The most time consuming part is mixing the egg with the oatmeal and the sugar
(memories of a little girl). Don't be discouraged because the end result is worth it!
Take 2 teaspoons of the dough and make walnut-sized piles on a buttered
and floured baking sheet or with parchment paper.
Bake at 180°C (gas mark 6) for about 10 minutes.
The sides of the cakes will turn brown, do not let the cakes get colored.

Vassiliki cookies with sesame seeds

Serves 4

Preparation time: 15 min

Ingredients

2 glasses of peanut oil
1 glass of granulated sugar
1 glass of dry white wine
1 glass of sesame
1kg of flour with yeast

Preparation

Preheat the oven to 180°C (thermostat 6).
Mix the oil with the sugar and the white wine, then add the flour and the sesame seeds.
Once the dough is ready, make small dough pieces in the shape of a little finger
and unite them to form dough snails.
Place the cookies on a baking sheet on which we have placed parchment
paper. Bake for about 15 minutes.
Accompanied by a coffee, delicious!

Yogurt and cookie cake

Serves 7

Preparation time: 20 min

Ingredients

2yoghurt
6pots of yogurtflour
3/4pot of powdered sugar
1 jar of yogurtand olive oil
3 eggs

10biscuits (large BN type)
1 sachet of yeast

Preparation

Preheat the oven to 180°C (fan assisted)
Mix the eggs, flour, yogurt, sugar, olive oil and yeast in a large bowl until you have a sticky dough.
In a smaller bowl, crumble the cookies by hand or with a fork.
Mix the cookies and the dough until you have a fairly homogeneous dough.
Place in a silicone pan (no need to butter) or in an ovenproof pan (pre-buttered).
Let cool and put in a dish.
Enjoy this good cake warm.

apple and chocolate chip muffins
Serves 12

Preparation time: 10 min

Ingredients

2 plain yogurt cups (one of the cups will be used as a measure)
2 jars of flour
1.5 jars of sugar
1 packet of vanilla sugar
1 packet of yeast
2 eggs
25g melted butter
1 apple
50g of chocolate
30g of flaked almonds

Preparation

Pour a yogurt in a ramekin.
Wash it.
Mix the flour with the sugar, the vanilla sugar and the yeast.
Add the eggs and the 2 yoghurts.
Mix well.
Incorporate the melted butter.
Pour this batter into silicone muffin cups.
Peel the apple and cut it into small cubes.
Spread the apple, the chips and the flaked almonds on the dough.
Bake at Th 6/180°C for about 20 minutes.

Quick trifle with pears and speculoos
people: 2

Preparation time: 10 min

Ingredients

2 natural sweetened yoghurts
10 speculoos
2 pears in syrup
Pecan nuts
Chocolate

Preparation

Preparation time : 10 min
Cooking time : 0
Ingredients (for 2 people):
Preparation:
Crush the speculoos and set aside.
Cut pears into small cubes.
Place crushed speculoos in the bottom of two wide glasses or bowls. Drizzle
a tablespoon of syrup over the pears.
Arrange half of the yoghurts.
Add half of the pear cubes, then the speculoos.
Repeat the operation: yoghurt (the other half), pears again and finish
with the remaining speculoos.
You can add melted chocolate and pecans on top at the very end, or
of course leave as is, it's simple, quick and delicious.

Pumpkin Halloween Cookie
Serves 8

Preparation time: 10 min

Ingredients

3/4 cup of butter
1 cup of brown sugar
2 eggs
1 cup of pumpkin puree
2 cups of flour
1 cup of raisins
1 teaspoon vanilla extract
1 packet of yeast
1 teaspoon cinnamon
1/2 teaspoon nutmeg
1/2 teaspoon cloves
1 pinch of salt

Preparation

In a bowl, mix the softened butter and sugar, then the eggs, vanilla and pumpkin puree.

In another bowl, mix the flour, yeast, spices and salt. Add to the first mixture
and mix in the raisins.
Bake in a greased springform pan for 15 minutes at 190°C.
The pumpkin can be cooked in milk and water for 15-20 min (check
with a knife that it is cooked and soft enough to puree!).

Light spiced shortbread (no eggs, no butter)

Serves 8

Preparation time: 15 min

Ingredients

300farina
5g of yeast
150g margarine
160g brown sugar
1 tablespoon of oil
2 tablespoons water
1 teaspoon gingerbread spice
drop of food coloring (optional)

Preparation

Whisk together the sugar and margarine.
Gradually add the flour and yeast, alternating with the tablespoons of water and oil.
If the dough is a little too sticky, add a little flour.
Place the dough in cling film in the fridge for 10 - 15 min.
Roll out and cut out with cookie cutters (e.g. dinosaurs with green colored
dough for a little boy's birthday).
Bake in a preheated oven for 10 min at 200°C.

Small almond cookies

Serves 4

Preparation time: 10 min

Ingredients

300g of almond powder
3 eggs
300g of flour
300g of powdered sugar
Vanilla extract

Preparation

Place the dry ingredients (flour, sugar, almond powder) in a bowl and mix well.
Add the three eggs and mix well. The dough should be left to rest in a cool place

for two hours (or even overnight), covered with a transparent film.
Preheat the oven to 200°C (thermostat 6/7).
Roll out the dough to a thickness of about 2 cm. Strive the surface with a fork (or make drawings, according to your inspiration), then gild with egg yolk.
Bake for 15 to 20 minutes (not too long, as these cookies are best when they are still soft inside).
Once cooked, remove from oven and cut into squares or other shapes.

Small butter cookies
cookies: 10

Preparation time: 15 min

Ingredients

300g of butter
250g caster sugar
250g of potato starch
200g almond powder
250g of flour
1 egg
2 pinches of vanilla sugar

Preparation

Mix the ingredients: butter, sugars, flour, egg, starch and almonds.
Put this dough in the meat grinder using the shapes for small cookies, i.e. Spritzbredle.
Put on a baking sheet and bake for about 20 min (their color should remain fairly light).

Pink cake (with sponge cake)
Serves 6

Preparation time: 30 min

Ingredients

300g of Reims cookies
125g of butter
100g of sugar
1 eggplant
125g almond powder
Rum
Chocolate for pastry

Preparation

Crush the cookies into powder. Mix them in a bowl with the almond powder and sugar.
Add the egg and melted butter, as well as the rum. Mix well to obtain a homogeneous paste. Butter or oil a cake tin and place the mixture in it.
Let it set in the refrigerator for about 12 hours.

Glaze with chocolate.

Chocolate and Shortbread Delight
Serves 6

Preparation time: 20 min

Ingredients

300g dark chocolate (minimum 50% cocoa)
180g of butter
5 eggs
200g sugar
4Spirit cookies (shortbread cakes)

Preparation

Preheat the oven to 160°C (gas mark 5-6).
Butter a cake tin.
Gently melt the chocolate and butter in pieces in a saucepan. Mix with a spatula
(the chocolate must have a smooth consistency).
In a bowl, break the eggs and add the sugar. Whisk with an electric
mixer for about 5 minutes until the mixture turns white.
Add a quarter of the melted chocolate, then gradually add the rest,
in small quantities, mixing gently with a spatula.
Break the cookies into pieces. Scatter them over the chocolate mixture and mix quickly.
Pour the chocolate mixture into the cake tin. Place in the oven and bake for
40 minutes at 160°C. Let cool 30 min, before unmoulding.
Present the cake, warm or cold.

-

Chocolate, kiwi and speculoos caissettes
20 caissettes: 1

Preparation time: 1 hour

Ingredients

300g of pastry chocolate
20cl of liquid fresh cream
3kiwis
5speculoos
3 teaspoons of powdered sugar

Preparation

For this recipe, you will need the following materials:
- paper or silicone baking trays
- 1 brush

First, prepare the boxes: cut the chocolate into coarse chips and
melt two thirds of them in a bain-marie.
Once it is melted, take the pan out of the water and add the remaining third
of the chips, mix well so that the chocolate is homogeneous.
Take a brush and gently paint the inside of the boxes with the melted chocolate.
(You don't want the chocolate to be too liquid).
Leave in the fridge for 20 minutes to harden.
Then apply a second layer and let it harden for another 20 minutes. You can add a third
layer if you are using large boxes, or if you feel that your first 2 layers are too thin.
For the kiwifruit-speculoos filling, dice three kiwifruit and let them drain for
a good 10 minutes with 2 teaspoons of sugar or powdered sugar.
Then collect the juice and thicken it in a saucepan over very low heat, adding
a little water if you don't get enough juice.
To assemble: very carefully remove the chocolate cases from
the molds (make sure your hands are cold).
Place the diced kiwis in the bottom of each case, cold.
Whip 20 cl of very cold fresh cream with a teaspoon of powdered sugar.
Top your cupcakes with whipped cream and serve with the kiwi coulis and speculoos crumbs.
You can make this recipe with any fruit and top it with coconut, caramel,
or whatever you think is good enough!

Basic recipe for cookies
cookies about: 40

Preparation time: 1h20

Ingredients

300g of flour
100g almond powder
150g of vergeoise (or sugar)
3 medium eggs
1/2 sachet of baking powder

Preparation

Preheat the oven to 180°C (gas mark 6).
Mix the flour with the sugar, the almond powder and the baking powder by hand or in a mixer.
Add the whole eggs and the ingredient of your choice (during the holidays
I add a gingerbread mix).
Let the dough rest for at least 1 hour in the refrigerator before cutting out your cookies (about
20, be careful of the thickness, depending on the size you choose) with a cookie cutter.
Place your cookies on a baking sheet lined with baking paper.
Bake for 10-20 minutes until golden brown. If you like them soft, place them in
the center or a little higher up on the rack if you want them crisp (watch them
carefully as it depends on the size and thickness of the cookies). Let them cool
outside the oven before removing them carefully from the baking sheet.

Chocolate shortbread cookies (Italian Canestrelli style)
Cookies: 40

Preparation time: 15 min

Ingredients

300g of flour
100g cornstarch
100g of brown sugar
100g cocoa powder
250g of butter
4 egg yolks
4 teaspoons vanilla extract
1 large pinch of salt
100g chocolate (milk or dark)
4 tablespoons of icing sugar for the finish

Preparation

Take out the butter beforehand to soften it.
In a large bowl, sift all the dry ingredients: flour, cornstarch, brown sugar, pinch of salt and cocoa. Make a well and add the egg yolks, vanilla extract and butter cut into pieces.
Using your fingertips, quickly knead the ingredients together until you have a smooth dough. Shape it into a ball and wrap it in cling film to let it rest for 1 hour in a cool place.
Preheat your oven to 170°C (thermostat 5-6).
Take the dough out of the fridge and flatten it with a rolling pin, placing it between two sheets of baking paper to obtain a dough of about 0.5 cm thick.
Cut small cookies with a 4 cm diameter cookie cutter and add 4/5 chocolate chips on each cookie.
Place them on the baking sheet where you have previously spread parchment paper.
(Space the cookies, they will increase slightly in size during baking).
Put the cookies in the oven and leave them for about 8 to 10 minutes, depending on the power of the oven.
Remove from the oven and let cool on a rack before peeling the shortbread from the paper and sprinkle with powdered sugar.

Imprint

Mindful Publishing
We help you to publish your book!

By

TTENTION Inc.
Wilmington - DE19806
Trolley Square 20c

Contact: mindful.publishing@web.de

Made in the USA
Middletown, DE
01 September 2022